THE LIFE AND TIMES OF ALLEN SHER

AN AUTOBIOGRAPHY

Life Stories Imprint
A Division of Magic Mountain Press
ISBN #978-0-9715946-6-1

Library of Congress Control Number 2013938402
First Edition, May 2013

Sher, Allen Arthur: born November 22,1921
died May 2, 2013

Other works by the author:
Historical Figures in Catullus, July 1942, Master's Thesis,
Graduate College, University of Nebraska
Folk and Square Dancing as Related to the Social Studies Unit in New York City Elementary Schools, 1963, Columbia University,
Dissertation Abstracts: Volume XXIV, No. 7, 1964
The Street Railways of Rutland, 1980, Monograph,
Rutland Historical Society, Volume X: No. 1, Vermont

Published by
Magic Mountain Press
P.O. Box 1933, Asheville NC 28802

Printed in the United States of America by Lightning Source, Inc.
Cover and Book Design by Studio Potpourri

DEDICATION

This book is dedicated to the family and friends of Allen Sher, and all those students over the many years touched by his life. Working with Allen to publish this manuscript gave me special insight into one man's journey, and it is one I shall never forget. His love of education, his passion for teaching, his commitment to his synagogue, the Temple Beth El of Laurelton, VT and later, the Temple Beth Ha Tephila in Asheville, NC, demonstrate the deep caring he shared with his community. He loved organizing Spelling Contests, his most recent was in March at an elementary school in Asheville. He loved serving children, which is why being a Kiwanian, as a member of several Kiwanis Clubs, fed his desire to make a difference in our world. We served with Allen for many years in the Kiwanis Club of Asheville, and his legacy lives on.

Allen was very humorous, as you will see from some of the stories shared in these pages, and the chapters on Vermont and North Carolina humor.

He was a devoted husband and father, dedicated teacher, dear friend, and servant for the greater good.

His humble example should inspire us all.

Karon Korp
President
Magic Mountain Press
April, 2013

TABLE OF CONTENTS

Growing Up in the Years of the Great Depression

I was born on November 22, 1921 in Beth Israel Hospital, Second Avenue and 15th Street in New York City. My mother had a semi-private room and the other person in the room with her was a black woman. As I was growing up and did something that annoyed my mother, she would scold me by saying, "In the hospital, I think they gave me the wrong baby". My brother, Jack, three years older than I, stood on the steps of our house in Bensonhurst and shouted, "My mother gots a baby".

My first four years are dim in my memory, but I do recall that in 1926 we lived at 813 Metropolitan Avenue in the Williamsburg section of Brooklyn. My parents had a dry goods store with three rooms behind the store. I was five years old and my brother, Jack, was eight. Two blocks from our store was an iron foundry. It was always hot in that building because they needed fires to make the steel red hot. It was dirty from the coal that the men had to shovel and they used to come into our store to buy black underwear and other clothing. There was a trolley car line that went on Metropolitan Avenue from the Williamsburg Bridge Plaza to 121st Street in Jamaica. Next door to us, at 811 Metropolitan Avenue, was Mr. Feinberg and his family. He was a tailor, made alterations and cleaned and pressed clothing for his customers.

On Sunday afternoons, when stores had to be closed, my family would walk to the movies at the Folly Theater, Graham

Avenue and Broadway. We sat in the balcony for 15 cents each, seeing a movie and a vaudeville show on their stage. On the way home, we'd stop at KAMINS Delicatessen on Graham Avenue for franks and beans. My mother used to walk to a pushcart market on Moore Street and I'd help carry the food home in shopping bags. One day, a man came by with a horse and wagon, selling long watermelons at 50 cents each. My father and Mr. Feinberg went outside to buy a watermelon. They spent some time studying the melons and thumping them to find one that was the juiciest. They paid 50 cents for the melon, cut it in half and we each had half of a large watermelon for 25 cents.

In 1927, I entered Kindergarten at P.S. 23, was promoted, and finished the first grade in June 1928. On Sundays during July and August, we'd go as a family to Brighton Beach. We did not have a car and we took the subway where fare was only 5 cents per person. We'd walk to the Graham Avenue station and take the 14th Street line into Union Square, Manhattan. We'd change trains and take the Brighton Express to Brighton Beach. We'd carry sandwiches in a shopping bag, plus towels and a blanket. After finding a place on the beach close to the water, we'd sit on the blanket and eat our lunch. Because there were many people on the beach, peddlers would walk up and down selling ice cream, candy, pretzels, and other goodies. We had to wait an hour before going into the ocean, and during this hour, Jack and I would dig holes in the sand or play with a ball. When we finished swimming, we'd dry off, put on our clothing over our bathing suits and walk on the boardwalk toward Coney Island. It was fun to look at the different rides, and Jack and I knew that our father would give us 5 cents each for a ride on the merry-go-round. At Nathan's, we'd eat hot dogs (5 cents each), hamburgers with onions (also 5 cents), enjoy a big glass of root beer (5 cents), and an ice cream cone of frozen custard (5cents!).

In September of 1928, I entered Grade 2, was promoted in February 1929 to Grade 3 and in June 1929, I was promoted to Grade 4.

Al Smith, a Democrat, and Herbert Hoover, Republican, ran for President in November 1928. There was a fierce rivalry in our neighborhood between the two political parties. On Election Day, people of our area made a bonfire where Bushwick Avenue, Maspeth Avenue, and Metropolitan Avenue come together in a triangle park. Adults, helped by children, gathered wooden fruit boxes and made a big bonfire at this intersection. As soon as the Fire Department came and put out the fire, the men poured gasoline over the blackened boxes and started the fire again. That was what the Bushwick people did to celebrate Election Day.

On May 11, 1929, my sister, Florence, was born at St. Catherine's Hospital on Bushwick Avenue. Business was bad in the store. Many customers would buy things and say, 'Put it on the book". When the Great Depression hit us, people didn't have money to pay their bills. We moved to 3195 Fulton Street, in East New York, under the Broadway-Brooklyn elevated line. Again, we had a dry goods store, with three rooms behind the store. I walked to Public School 65 on Richmond Street for grades 4, 5 and 6. The store was not supposed to be open on Sundays but we kept the store open because we did business with people who were going to church and needed something. One Sunday, a policeman came into the store and threatened my mother with a ticket for having the store open. She was behind the counter, holding the baby, Florence, in her arms and she told him we were poor and needed the business. The policeman did not give her a ticket and thereafter, we remained closed on Sundays.

When I was 10, I had the idea of selling lollipops on the weekdays. I bought Charms lollipops wholesale in a store on the East Side. There were 144 lollipops in a box and the wholesale price was .75. I walked on the sand at Brighton Beach calling out, "Charms lollipops, penny-a-piece". Parents would beckon to me that they wanted lollipops and when I approached, the children wanted to know what flavors I had. A box contained orange, strawberry, chocolate, lemon and lime, and I'd keep selling until the lollipops were all gone. My profit was .69 for each gross I sold and

3

if I sold four boxes, I'd have $2.76 that I gave to my parents.

In 1931, we moved to 2354 Pitkin Avenue, between Ashford and Warwick Streets. This was in another section of East New York but we still lived on a street that had an elevated line running on it. This was the Fulton Street El that ran from Lefferts Avenue in Queens to Park Row, Manhattan. The nearest station was Linwood Street, three and a half blocks east. We never had an auto and to travel anyplace for business or pleasure, we'd take the trolley, bus, El, or subway. Until 1948, the fare was only 5 cents to go anywhere in the five Boroughs of New York City. You could even obtain a free transfer and go from one trolley to another or from one bus to another. I went to Junior High School 64 at Belmont Avenue and Berriman Street for grades 7A and 7B. Again, we had a dry goods store with three rooms behind the store. Next door to us was an Italian-American grocery. We bought milk there, using our own milk can, for 6 cents a quart. After one year at Jr. High School 64, my mother suggested that I go to Jr. High School 149 at Sutter Avenue and Wyona Street. I went there from February 1932 to June 1933 to study Latin and French. I'd always take lunch in a paper bag and because we were permitted to leave the school for lunch, some boys would go to a delicatessen for a hot dog or sandwich. Around the corner from the school on Wyona Street was a store where a woman sold potato knishes. She made them by hand, round and flat, and put them in a big pot of hot oil until they browned. Her knishes were 3 cents each or two for a nickel.

Graduation exercises were at Loews Premier, on Sutton Avenue and Hinsdale Street. Children dressed up for graduation but we were still suffering from the Depression and my parents did not have money to buy me a pair of new shoes. My mother bought new shoes for me but they were second-hand shoes from a shoemaker near Blake Avenue. He had a rack of unclaimed shoes and there was a pair of black shoes that fit me. They had new soles, new rubber heels, and a high polish. They cost 50 cents and I was happy with them. There are five songs that I remember and one of them was a lively song we sang at Jr. High School 149:

4

"1-4-9 is the school for me,
Drives away all adversity,
Steady and true, we'll be to you,
Loyal to 1-4-9-, RAH! RAH! RAH!
Raise on high the red and white,
Praise it with all your might,
Steady and true we'll be to you ,
Loyal to 1-4-9"

The music teacher at 149 was Mrs. Phillips. We would report to the Auditorium for Music and Mrs. Phillips was able to play piano and handle three classes at one time. She taught us patriotic songs, spirituals, holiday songs, and occasionally, a song for fun. One song that she taught us was "Stout Hearted Men". This was a lively song ("Give me some men who are stout-hearted men, and I'll soon give you 10,000 more") and when we learned the popular part, she taught us the song's introduction. It began with, "You, who have dreams, if you act, they will come true…". At one time she played the introduction on the piano, meaning for us to listen to the intro and sing when she nodded her head. I thought she meant that we should sing the intro and I sang out with a loud, "You who have dreams…". She stopped, stood, and asked, "Who did that?" I raised my hand because I thought I was doing the right thing. She made me come up to the front of the auditorium and sit under the baby grand piano. At the end of the period, she scolded me again and ordered me to bring my mother to school. My mother obeyed the teacher's request and went to see her at the school. The problem was ironed out and I never caused trouble after that.

Because business again was bad, we had to close the store. We moved to 483 Cleveland Street, between Pitkin Avenue and Belmont Avenue, and had an apartment on the ground floor for $25 a month. We had trouble paying the rent on time and my mother would send me to the landlord with a five dollar bill to pay the rent in installments. She always warned me, "Be sure to get a receipt for the money." Because of the apartment houses on this block, there were children of all ages living on Cleveland Street. We played street games that cost little or no money and the boys and girls on our block didn't get into trouble with these games, which included: Kick the can, hit the bat, dodge ball, elbow wrestling, actors and actresses, checkers, box ball, Chinese tag, dominoes, Johnny on the pony, stick ball, baseball off the wall, races: running, walking, skipping, hopping, marbles, scavenger hunt, three steps to Germany, skelly, ring-a-leaveeo, punch ball, potsy, hide and seek, bounce the ball and hit the penny, playing cards: war, casino, and Old Maid.

We also collected the cards that came in packages of gum and the covers of Dixie cups of ice cream that had Hollywood stars under the lids. There were games that we played with these cards such as: off the wall, tossing cards, to be closest to the wall, and matching the cards your opponent tossed. When we were older, we played table games like Candy Land, Sorry, Chutes and Ladders, and Honest John.

We went to WISOTSKY'S Bakery, on Sutter Avenue and Warwick Street, for rolls that were 3 for 5 cents, and for rye bread and pumpernickel. I would go shopping with my mother to the Blake Avenue pushcart market. We would walk from Linwood Street to Warwick Street to see who had the cheapest prices for apples, oranges, string beans, lettuce, beets, and other fruits and vegetables. She patronized one butcher who used to have a special on lamb stew, 5 cents/lb. or 6 lbs. for a quarter. There was a fish store on Cleveland Street and Blake Avenue, where my mother would buy cod fish or haddock and cut it into very thin slices.

When I was graduated from Jr. High School 149, I went to Thomas Jefferson High School. For the third and fourth terms, I went to the Thomas Jefferson Annex on Belmont Avenue and Sackman Street. It was 25 blocks from home but I walked each way. In bad weather, my mother gave me a nicket to take the Pitkin Avenue bus to school. I always walked home. Jefferson was a big school and had 3,000 students. I was never absent, and never late, and each term I received a Certificate of Honor for such good attendance and punctuality. I was graduated from Thomas Jefferson High School in June 1936 at the Brooklyn Academy of Music in downtown Brooklyn. My mother and father attended the graduation exercises. They took the Fulton Street El to Lafayette Avenue and then walked to the Academy of Music. One of the songs we sang at our High School graduation was our Alma Mater:

> *"We have taken from the woodland,*
> *Autumn's golden hues,*
> *And the blue of midnight heaven,*
> *For our colors true.*
> *Lift that banner,*
> *Lift it skyward,*
> *Let our praise be true; Jefferson,*
> *Our Alma Mater, The orange and the blue."*

Early in 1936, we moved to a second floor apartment at 296 Pennsylvania Avenue. My father took out a pushcart of bananas or other fruit every day from Monday through Friday. On Saturdays, he would rent two pushcarts: one for him and one that Jack and I would use. We would walk with our pushcarts to Ozone Park and Richmond Hill to sell bananas. I'd go from door to door selling bananas, 10 cents a dozen for medium sized bananas and 6 for 10 cents for large bananas. At the end of the day, we'd go home with any fruit we hadn't sold and then return the pushcart to Simon, who had a yard on Elton Street between Blake and Dumont Avenues. Simon would give us straw so we wouldn't bruise the bananas and we paid him 15 cents a day for renting the pushcart. My sister, Florence, was seven years old and sometimes I'd give her a ride in the pushcart, sitting on the straw.

On Mother's Day, Jack and I would make a few dollars by selling artificial flowers outside St. Jerome's R.C. Church. We had paper carnations and would sell them for 10 cents each, pink if your mother was alive, and white if your mother had died. The church had three masses on Sunday mornings and we'd usually sell all of our flowers on those Sundays. We'd make $3. or $4. on a Sunday morning and give that money to our folks.

Another day when we made a few dollars was Memorial Day. Jack and I would go to Eastern Parkway in Brooklyn where there was a parade starting at 11:00AM. It went from Utica Avenue to Grand Army Plaza and there were always crowds of parents and children to see the action. We would walk along the parkway selling U.S. flags to children who were there to watch the parade. When the parade ended, we walked to Myrtle Avenue and took the Myrtle Avenue EL to Metropolitan Avenue in Middle Village in Queens. Many Italian people would go to cemeteries to visit their family plots on Memorial Day. We would stand outside of St. John's Cemetery and sell U.S. and Italian flags to people who were going into the cemetery to decorate the graves of their families. We sold them at 15 cents each, or two for a quarter.

In the summer of 1935, I was 13 years old and anxious to make some money for our family. Jack worked in Manhattan on Ann Street near City Hall in a store that sold books and used magazines. Next to the store where he worked was a stand with a huge sign: JUMBO MALTED MILK IN A JUMBO GLASS WITH ICE CREAM – 5 cents. Jack asked me if I wanted to work for the two men who ran this stand and my job was to wash the glasses. I'd make $1.00 a day which came to $5 a week. I took the job with the bonus that if I wanted a malted, I could make one for myself, at no charge. Everything went well – I washed the glasses as fast as I could so the men could make malteds for the customers. Sometimes I served a customer who, rushing up to the counter, would say, "Gimme a malted!" and I'd respond, "What flavor?" The customer would reply, "What flavors do you have?". I'd say, "Chocolate, vanilla, strawberry, cherry, …". One day the boss took me aside and advised me, "If someone asks for a malted, say 'Chocolate?'" Nine times out of ten, he'll say ,"Yes" and this saved time.

In June 1936, my father went back into business and opened a Variety Store at 2682 Pitkin Avenue, between Chestnut and Doscher Streets. As with the other stores, there was a three room apartment behind the store. It was under the Chestnut Street station of the Fulton Street EL and it was a fairly busy street with people going to, or coming from, the trains. We sold magazines and books, school supplies, some dry goods , greeting cards, and Christmas decorations, etc.

In the summer of 1936, I was a high school graduate and I obtained a job as a counselor at the Manhattan Beach Day Camp. The camp had many school buses that covered Brooklyn, calling for children, taking them to the Day Camp for swimming and other activities, and then taking the children home again about 5:00PM. I earned $50 for the two summer months and I enjoyed the work, which put me in the water swimming with my eight campers.

Opposite our store was a small A & P. We used to watch their specials and walk across the street to buy items that were on sale. They sold canned salmon, and a one pound can of the A & P brand sold for 13 cents , or 2 for a quarter. Every Thursday night, my mother made a large salmon salad, using two cans of salmon. She always cut onions into the salad and we had a good healthy dish that was also cheap. Mom used to make potato latkes on Thursdays. Potatoes were cheap at 20 lbs. for a quarter, and she used a hand grater to shred the potatoes. Next to the A & P was a German Bakery. My mother would send me over to buy mixed buns which were 3 for a nickel. She told me to ask if they had any day-old items and if so, it was always half price for those cakes. The day-old buns were 10 cents a dozen and we enjoyed them because they were cheaper.

When the summer of 1936 ended, so did my job as a counselor at the Day Camp. I planned to go to the evening session of Brooklyn College in downtown Brooklyn, so I looked for a daytime job. Through an employment agency, I found that the DIENSTAG Feather Company, on West 8th and Mercer Street, needed a delivery boy. The salary was $8.00 a week. I went to Mr. DIENSTAG for the job. He said he could only pay $7.00. I took the job and delivered feathers and quills and ornaments for ladies' hats to manufacturers in that area of Manhattan. When I returned from one delivery, there was usually another to go. If I had to wait for another shipment of feathers, Mr. Dienstag hollered, "SWEEP THE FLOOR!" I lasted one week at this job and had to pay the employment agency 10%, or 70 cents .

CHAPTER 2

College and a University

In the fall of 1936, I started my studies at Brooklyn College, taking two courses in the morning. My mother advised me to look for another job in the HELP WANTED columns of the New York Times. I came across an ad where a company was looking for messengers. It was the Service Messenger Company, located at 55 W. 42nd Street, across from Bryant Park. The job paid $6 a week, working from 9 to 5, five days a week. I took the job, because when I left work at 5:00, I could go to downtown Brooklyn to take two courses at Brooklyn College. As a messenger, most of the deliveries were in the office buildings of Midtown Manhattan, but occasionally, there were trips to other boroughs and to New Jersey. The company rule stipulated that if the errand was within 12 blocks or less from our office, we'd walk. If the destination was more than 12 blocks, we would receive a nickel to take the bus or subway. At that time, President Franklin D. Roosevelt urged the Congress to pass Social Security legislation, and Congress did pass it in 1936. It went into effect on January 1, 1937 and my boss took 1% out of my salary and paid it into the Social Security fund. The deduction of 6 cents each week was taken from my pay check and it was to be matched by the employer. Halfway through the year, my boss asked me to come in on Saturdays from 9:00AM to 1:00PM. He raised our salary to $7.00 per week and the deduction for Social Security became 7 cents/week.

As mentioned earlier, my brother, Jack, worked in a store in New York City that sold books and magazines. With his knowledge of this business, my folks changed from a store with just dry goods to a place where people came in for a variety of needs. I went to a junk shop on Atlantic Avenue and Essex Street where they paid .35 cents for 100lbs. of paper and magazines. When the junk dealer baled the paper, he would put aside pulp magazines such as The Shadow, Doc Savage, Sport Stories, and smooth paper magazines like Redbook, Cosmopolitan, and Good Housekeeping. I'd go through the magazines and pick the ones we could sell. I paid .01 cent each for the magazines and we sold them for .05 and .10 cents. Since we had no car, I'd take the magazines in two big bundles, walk with them one long block to Liberty Avenue, take the Bergen Street Trolley to Chestnut Street, and then walk two long blocks to our store on Pitkin Avenue.

Bergen Street Line Trolley Car Brooklyn

My father would go to the wholesalers on the Lower East Side and buy the other items we could sell. The variety of things we carried became known in the neighborhood and we began to do business as Sher's Variety Store. We kept a poster in the window of our store advertising the movies that were playing at the R.K.O. Bushwick. They changed the posters weekly and as they did that, they gave us a free pass to the theater. Jack or I would use it and we saw good movies, free of charge.

In the Spring Semester of 1937, I continued in the evening division of Brooklyn College and took three courses: Latin, College Algebra, and Spanish. Brooklyn College had rooms in five office buildings in downtown Brooklyn, and we had to rush from one building to another to make it to class on time. It was in my first year that I learned:

"From the portals of Joralemon,
To a class at Willoughby,
Then we tramp out once again, what fun,
Up to Pearl for history.
Through a maze of trolley cars we dodge,
Right by traffic cops we charge – and take – our chances.
From the portals of Joralemon,
To a class at Willoughby."

In 1941, when I was a senior, I learned the Alma Mater. The words were written by Sylvia Fine Kaye, the wife of Danny Kaye, and the music was by Robert Friend.

Though These May Not Be Towr's of Marble

"Though these may not be towr's of marble
Lifting white spires in air,
Oh, Brooklyn is our Alma Mater,
And she is wondrous fair.
Within the gray halls ever lit,
The lamps of learning burn
And even on to goals of glory
Young eager spirits yearn.

Although the walls are not of silver,
Golden the laughter rings,
To stars above we turn our faces
Soaring on sweeping wings.
Our friendship here is wov'n with learning,
Joy fills all our days.
So hail to thee, our Alma Mater;
Brooklyn, we sing thy praise"

13

I recall that I was taking, in the summer of 1937, a required three credit evening course at Brooklyn College, called Introduction to Government. The text was a great big thick book by Ogg and Ray, and I remember that people would look at me as I sat in the subway, reading and taking notes from the huge text.

When summer came, I worked full time for the Blaine-Thompson Advertising agency, at 321 W. 44th Street in New York City as an errand boy for $15 a week. One day the manager of the office had a bad cold. He sent me to the drug store for a bottle of REM, the Remarkable Remedy. I gave it to him and he took a sip, then drank half the bottle. He seemed to like it and sent me out for another bottle. Afterwards, I learned that one of the chief ingredients of REM was alcohol.

The Fall of 1937 was a history-making time because Brooklyn College was building a new campus in Flatbush at Bedford Avenue and Avenue H. This would require the closing of the five buildings it had been using in downtown Brooklyn. Because the new buildings in Flatbush were able to accommodate more students, I transferred to the Day Session. My parents didn't have any money to send me to college but tuition at Brooklyn was free and I only had to pay a Registration Fee and for textbooks. With the money that I had saved, we managed it. Most students of Brooklyn College did not have autos. We took the IRT Subway to Flatbush Avenue or the BMT to Avenue H and then walked to the college. Some students came by bus or trolley car. I used to take the Fulton Street EL to Franklin Avenue, then Shuttle to Prospect Park, and then the Brighton Beach Local to Avenue H. It used to take one hour to go from home to college but the fare was only a nickel. Because of the courses I had taken in the evening sessions, I had earned enough credits to register as a sophomore. On weekends, I worked at Ebbets Field, Yankee Stadium, and the Polo Grounds selling football souvenirs.

There were extra curricular activities at Brooklyn College and I became interested in Gilbert and Sullivan and joined the G & S Society at the College. We'd meet every Wednesday from 12:00 to 2:00, and we'd socialize and sing choruses and solos from the

14

different comic operas. I borrowed books from the library and learned more about the lives of Gilbert & Sullivan and their works. I used to copy on index cards the lyrics of some of the solos, duets, and choruses. At home, I'd listen to the music played on the radio by WNYC and I'd sit next to the radio whenever they played music by the talented duo. Every spring, Brooklyn College would have a Country Fair and our G & S Society would present a program of music from different operas. I became friendly with Ruth Steiner through a mutual fondness of Gilbert & Sullivan.

Ruth wanted to become a high school teacher of English, I wanted to become a high school teacher of Latin and this, too, created a friendship where we began going steady. As seniors, we became student teachers and Ruth did her assignment in English at Midwood High School while I taught Latin at James Madison High School.

Since 1940 was a Leap Year, the G & S Society took a special interest in the "Pirates of Penzance". When Gilbert wrote the libretto in 1880, his story involved Frederic, a pirate who was born in a leap year and would not reach the age of 21 until 1940. Because of this occurrence on February 29, 1940, WNYC allowed us to do a half hour presentation of the "Pirates" on that date. We all took the subway to the studios of WNYC and did our program of solos and choruses. Ruth sang a solo, "When Frederic was a little lad", and I sang the policeman's solo, "When a felon's not engaged in his employment." Stanley Sontag was the regular pianist at our Wednesday meeting and he played the accompaniment for us when we performed on the radio.

In the summer of 1940, I worked full time again for the Blaine-Thompson Company. Ruth worked as a counselor for a camp in New Jersey, and since we were going steady, we wrote letters to each other daily. I had my first date with Ruth in December of 1940. Theodore Roosevelt High School in the Bronx was presenting the Gilbert & Sullivan opera, "Patience." I obtained two tickets for it and when I called for Ruth at her apartment house, at 1417 Avenue K in Brooklyn, we took the subway to the Lower

15

East Side. We went to YONAH SCHIMMEL'S KNISHE Bakery on Houston Street and had knishes for supper. From Houston Street, we took the E train to the Bronx and saw a very entertaining performance of "Patience" with musical accompaniment by the High School Band.

At the recommendation of Dr. Alice KOBER, our teacher of Latin at Brooklyn College, three students who were majoring in Latin went to Baltimore during Christmas week to attend the annual convention of teachers of Latin. Seymour SCHNEID, Edward SHACK, and I took her advice and went to Baltimore for this meeting. Afterwards, I followed up by writing to one of the speakers, Dr. Michael GINSBURG, of the University of Nebraska. He encouraged me to come to Lincoln to study Latin there and he also suggested that I apply for a graduate assistant position. After talking this over with my parents, I applied for the opportunity and was accepted. To serve as an assistant, I had to teach Latin to undergraduate students and to serve as a Librarian in the Classics Department Library. I would receive $400 for the academic year plus free tuition for the courses I had to take for an M.A. My mother and father encouraged me to become a teacher and I accepted a position, planning to go to Nebraska from Sept. 1941 to June of 1942. In my last semester at Brooklyn College, I did student teaching at James Madison High School and found that I enjoyed the experience of teaching.

From February 1st to August 15th of 1941, I worked for Warner Brothers in their Mailroom, handling all kinds of incoming and outgoing mail. Graduation from Brooklyn College took place on June 15th. My mother and father closed the store and took the trains to attend the exercises on campus.

In September of 1941, I left for Nebraska by Greyhound Bus. The fare was $29, and was cheaper than railroad fare which was $55. It took 48 hours by bus but it stopped regularly for meals. I slept on the bus and carried all of my possessions in one valise and one carton. On reaching Lincoln, I confirmed all of the details of my new position as an assistant, making sure that I would receive $40 per month from the University, and free tuition towards an M.A.

At the Student Union building, I met three Easterners: Harry Cohen (a graduate assistant in the Department of Geography, from Worcester MA), Albert Chicofsky (a junior in the Dental School, from Boston) and Irving Zass (a senior in Entomology, also from Boston). The four of us rented a two room furnished apartment for $24 a month, at 1621 Q Street, in Lincoln. It had four desks, two double beds, and a tiny kitchen. We each paid $6 a month for the rent. I took graduate courses in Latin, taught undergraduate courses, served as Librarian in the Classical Library, and I prepared to write a thesis on, Rhetorical Figures of Speech in Catullus. On Sundays, I taught Grade 4 in the Religious School of the Jewish synagogue. In Lincoln, any part time job for college students paid "2 bits an hour", so working in the religious school from 9:30 – 12:30, I received 75 cents each Sunday. At the end of the month, the Sisterhood gave me a check for $3.00. The Temple had a Passover Seder and, as a fringe benefit, they invited me to attend free of charge.

On Thanksgiving weekend, I took the Greyhound Bus to visit my Aunt Mae and Uncle Rob in Chicago. He took me sightseeing and we went on a tour of the Swift Meat Packing Plant (in the stockyards) and a tour of the Ford Assembly Plant. I saw the way that hogs, cattle and sheep were killed and how the meat was produced. It was most interesting to see a Ford car being put together in a half hour. We saw the body lifted into place on the assembly line, the different workers performing their tasks, and how at the end of 30 minutes, a man sat down behind the wheel, inserted the key in the ignition, turned on the motor, and drove the car into the parking lot.

Whenever the University of Nebraska football team played a home game in Lincoln, I saw it because I had bought a season ticket. At these games, we sang, "There Is No Place Like Nebraska"

17

to the accompaniment of the University of Nebraska Band. The song went like this,

"There is no place like Nebraska,
Good old Nebraska U.,
The girls are the fairest,
The boys are the squarest,
Of any school that you knew.
There is no place like Nebraska,
Where they're all true blue,
We'll all stick together,
Like good friends forever,
At dear old Nebraska U."

On one weekend, the football team was going to play in Minnesota. There was a big parade to accompany the team to the railroad station where they would take the north bound train. On that Saturday afternoon, I went for a haircut. The barber was listening to the game on the radio and I was concerned that he not become too excited as he used the scissors and razor on me.

One Saturday night, I had a date with Ethel May Lewis. Ethel May was a Latin major and a graduate assistant, just as I was, in the Classics Department. She came from Council Bluffs, Iowa and was a graduate of Creighton University. We walked to the Cornhusker Hotel, the largest hotel in Lincoln, and spent the evening with beer and popcorn. Beer was 5 cents a glass and popcorn was 5 cents for a big bowl. We had a pleasant evening talking about our backgrounds, our work in Lincoln, and what lay ahead.

In our apartment, we each had a desk and we all studied diligently. Occasionally, late in the evening, when someone was really hungry, we'd walk down O Street to Pete's Chili Parlor. We'd buy a frank in a roll with chili and onions – a good deal at 5 cents each.

For June and July, I had found a room in a boarding house where I paid $7 per month. To help pay that rent, I looked for a job and I could have had one, working for an undertaker, answering the phone at night. I didn't take it. Instead, I did find one, working as assistant fry cook in the snack bar of the Student Union building. We did a big business in hamburgers and part of my job was to toast the hamburger buns before we put on the meat. My job again paid "two bits an hour".

When I finished my thesis, I submitted it to Professor Lowe, Professor Forbes, and Professor Ginsburg for their review. I had to take an oral examination before these members of the Classics Department and I sweated through this stage of the Master's Degree. After questioning me for a half-hour, they asked me to step out while they pondered their decision. Professor Forbes came out with a smile on his face and his right arm extended. "Congratulations, Mr. Sher", he announced, "you're a Master of Arts."

When WWII started with the bombing of Pearl Harbor on December 7th, 1941, the United States government sold war bonds to help finance the war. A bond cost $18.75 and when it matured, it was worth $25.00. If you did not have the money to buy a bond, you could buy .10 or .25 stamps at the post office and paste them in an album they gave you. When I received my monthly check of $40, I would cash it and buy two or three stamps towards a war bond. It was the best I could do to help my country at that time.

With my M.A. diploma in hand, I returned to New York City. There were no jobs for teachers of Latin but I did obtain a job as a shipping clerk for HALPERN & CHRISTENFELD, at 19th Street between Fifth and Sixth Avenues in Manhattan. This company made jodhpurs and riding habits for people who went horseback riding but when WWII started, the company shifted to making military uniforms. At a salary of $21 a week, I helped with incoming and outgoing shipments and handled clothing that was made by women working at their sewing machines. The Branch Trucking Company handled crates of merchandise for us. Our company was on the 8th floor of the building, and we had to use the freight elevator to move the cartons and crates. I helped Pete, the truck driver for Branch, loading and unloading our items. One day, Pete said, "Hey, Allen, do you like pecans?" "Yes", I answered. In the truck, he had six burlap bags of pecans that he had brought up from Georgia. He used his baling hook, put a hole in one of the bags and gave me a paper bag full of pecans. He explained to me, "You can't help it if a bag tears in transit". I worked at Halpern & Christenfeld until I was drafted in 1943.

My sister, Florence, went to the High School of Music and Art in Manhattan from 1942-1946. These were the years of WW II and everything in life seemed secondary to our government's needs for money, soldiers, ammunition, and equipment to fight the war. When she was graduated from High School, she went to Queens College and received a B.A. in 1948. She was interested in social work and she worked in a hospital on Welfare Island as a medical social worker. She returned to higher education in 1965 by going to CCNY and received an M.A. in 1974. Florence then worked at the ISABELLA HOUSE in Upper Manhattan as a Social Worker. She was able to go to Hunter College and she became a Doctor of Social Work in 1972.

CHAPTER 3

World War II

When World War II started, I had to register with the Draft Board. They classified me as 1-A and I was drafted on February 12, 1943. I passed the physical examination, even though the doctor told me I had a deviated septum. I was inducted one week later and on February 19th, I was sent to Camp Upton, way out on the eastern part of Long Island, in Yaphank. They assigned me to the Fifth Receiving Company. We slept in a tent, with a pot-bellied stove in the center, for 12 days. It was COLD and the other soldiers called us the Frozen Fifth. I took the Army Aptitude Test and told the interviewing officer of my education and experience. He put me in the Signal Corps and gave me the classification of 808, cryptanalyst. The lieutenant explained that our radio men would intercept Japanese weather reports and turn them over to us. Our job was to break the Japanese code and then give that weather information to our forecasters. Our weather men would combine the Japanese weather with reports from our own weather stations and tell our pilots where to fly in Manchuria and Japan and where to drop bombs.

After being at Camp Upton for 12 days, another soldier and I received orders to go to Washington, DC. The Army has to feed its soldiers and they gave us a bag lunch to eat on the train. We took the Long Island Railroad to Pennsylvania Station in Manhattan and then carrying our two barracks bags, we found the platform for the train to D.C. The Pennsylvania Railroad took us to Union Station, and upon arriving, I showed my orders to the military police in the station. One soldier called the base in Arlington, VA, where I was supposed to report. The motor pool sent a jeep to drive me to the Army base there. The base turned out to be Arlington Hall, a private school that was taken over by the Army Signal Corps. The quarters were very comfortable and on Saturday, after we passed Inspection, we were allowed to swim in their indoor pool. The water was delightfully warm and green and I didn't waste any time before diving into the water. I hadn't looked to see which end was SHALLOW and which end was DEEP. I dived into the shallow end and my head hit the tiled floor of the pool. I stood up in two feet of water, dazed and confused because of a bump on the right side of my forehead. When I touched the bump, I felt blood, and decided I should go to the Infirmary. Sgt. Greene was the man on duty and after examining my wound, he put some antiseptic on the area and covered it with a bandage. I found out later that Sgt. Greene had been an embalmer in civilian life. If a medical doctor had treated me, I think he would have taken a few stitches to close the area. To this day, I have a scar over my right eye to remind me of the dive into the pool of Arlington Hall.

The Army sent me to VINT HILL FARMS, Warrenton, VA, about 40 miles west of Washington, for basic training. I spent three months at Vint Hill Farms, hiking, receiving target practice, and learning how to become a soldier. In addition to the outdoor exercises, we had classroom training in cryptography. This was the way in which we sent weather reports, telling of wind speed, cloud formations, and other observations.

One day, our sergeant told us that the Red Cross was sending a bloodmobile to collect blood donations. "I want all you men", he roared, "to sign up to donate because when you go overseas, you may need that blood". I gave a pint of blood at that time and have since given blood on 87 other occasions. In December of 1993, I went to donate blood in Hendersonville, NC, but I was rejected because of a new pill I was taking and it was affecting my blood.

88 pints of blood means 11 gallons that I have given to the Red Cross and I have always been thankful that I was able to help others in this way. The Red Cross gave me a gold gallon pin in the shape of a drop of blood and I wear it proudly with the number 11 below it.

From Virginia, the Army sent me to the Overseas Replacement Training Center at Seymour Johnson Field, in Goldsboro, North Carolina. At this field, I was transferred to the Air Corps because the Army told me that obtaining Japanese weather would help our pilots. This was true because when I was sent to a B-29 base near CHENGTU, CHINA, we did intercept Japanese weather observations and we gave that information to our forecasters.

One Saturday afternoon, I went into Goldsboro and walked up and down Main Street to see the city's attractions. I passed the movie theater and noticed the box office where they sold tickets. It was V- Shaped and on one side, they sold tickets to WHITES and on the other side, tickets to BLACKS. This was surprising but coming from the north, I had never experienced that form of segregation.

I had a weekend pass from Seymour Johnson Field and on Saturday I took the train to New York City to see the family and my fiancée, Ruth Steiner. Since I had to return to the air base by 0800 on Monday, I left Pennsylvania Station on Sunday at 3 PM. All seats were taken and I stood for four hours. At D. C., everybody left the car and I sat in a seat enjoying the opportunity to sit and stretch. This train was continuing south, and was going to Richmond, VA.. The conductor told me I had to move forward to another car because south of DC, this car was "for colored". Here was another example of segregation that we had never seen up north.

From Goldsboro, we went by troop train to Norfolk, VA to board our ship for overseas. I was one of a group of 10 soldiers who had received training as Cryptanalysts. We were being sent to the China-Burma-India theater of operations to help our weather forecasters with their predictions. The ship, the Empress of Japan, had been a passenger liner of Canada, traveling between Vancouver and Tokyo and it had been converted to a troop ship for soldiers. Our cabin was on D deck, as low down in the ship as possible. There were 12 bunks in this cabin and we occupied three walls, each four bunks high. The Special Services Department had left recreational equipment on one of the bunks and our men helped themselves to decks of cards, checkerboards, and checkers, dominoes, and other games. I was the last man into the cabin and the only item for me was a cribbage board.

I learned how to play cribbage, and am continuing to play cribbage to this date. It is an excellent game for two people and I learned that it is very popular in Alaska. Gold was discovered in SE Alaska in 1880 in the Klondike district of the Yukon region of Canada. This caused the GOLD RUSH where men hoped to find gold. Many times, a pair of men would work together all day, prospecting for gold. At sundown they would retire to their tents, light a candle, and eat their supper. After supper, they would play cribbage and it became so popular that souvenir shops in Alaska sell cribbage boards of all sizes and shapes. My wife and I played cribbage at home and cribbage when we went on vacation trips. In 2010, I found a cribbage group in Asheville that meets every Monday at 6 PM. There are some 30 people in the group and we pair off to play and enjoy cribbage, a game that I first learned in World War II.

In 1943, the Mediterranean Sea had many German submarines and rather than go to India pursued by enemy subs, our ship went from Norfolk, south to Capetown, South Africa. While the ship was being refueled at Capetown, we had one day of shore leave. We were able to explore Table Mountain and other points of interest, plus eating comfortably in Capetown's restaurants. We left South Africa, sailed between Mozambique and Madagascar, and then northeast across the Indian Ocean to Bombay. The trip took 28 days and we reached Bombay, India in January, 1944.

From Bombay, we went by railroad to Karachi, India, and then to New Delhi, the capital of the CBI(China-Burma-India) area

Copies of letters Allen sent home to his family during World War II of the war. We spent 10 months in New Delhi, doing the work of Signal Corps Intelligence. Since there was a lot of malaria in India, we slept under netting to keep the mosquitoes from attacking us. We received orders to fly into China but I caught impetigo when I went to an Indian barber for a haircut. The medics put me in the hospital and applied yellow sulfur ointment to the sores on my face. Temperature was 110° and I developed fever blisters because of the heat. They applied a brownish tannic acid to the heat blisters and for 10 days, my face was a mess. When I left the hospital, I followed the other cryptanalysts to Calcutta, Assam, and over the Himalayas, in a two engine C-47 to KUNMING, China, and then to a B-29 base at Chengtu. We were part of the 10th Weather Squadron, providing weather information for our pilots. The B-29's were the biggest bombers we had and they made bombing raids over Manchuria and Japan, helped by the weather information we provided about Japanese weather.

Of three CBI incidents that I remember vividly, two are experiences in India and one was in China. In April, 1944, the Jewish Chaplain made arrangements for us to have a Passover Seder in New Delhi. He reserved the second floor banquet room of a hotel in New Delhi for us and obtained as many Passover items as possible. From the Jewish Welfare Board, he had matzohs sent to us, together with HAGADAHS and kosher wine. About 40 Jewish soldiers attended and participated in the Passover readings and rituals. Nearby was a plate of matzos. I asked a waiter, "Bearer, may we have more matzos?" He said, "Yes, Sahib", went into the kitchen and returned without any matzos. He stood against the wall, arms folded across his chest, and I asked him again, "Bearer, may we have more matzos?" Again he replied, "Yes, Sahib", went into the kitchen and returned once more without matzos. I said again, "Bearer, may we have more matzos?" At the far end of the table, I saw a plate with one matzo and I pointed to it. His face broke into a big smile and he said, "BISCUITS, Sahib!" He went into the kitchen and this time brought a plate of matzos for us.

In June, 1944, we were told to go to a theater in New Delhi to see a British training film. At the door was a SIKH soldier, in full military uniform asking, "Pass, Sahib?" Nobody had given us a pass, but I had to do something. I took out my wallet and showed him my BEER RATION CARD. The guard nodded and opened the door for us to enter.

In October, 1944, we were at a B-29 base near CHENGTU, China. Yom Kippur, the most important holiday of the Jewish people, was approaching and the Jewish soldiers obtained a room where we could have a KOL NIDRE service at 8 PM. I arrived at 7:30 with my helmet and machine gun. The Chinese knew that Japanese were flying toward us. There was an immediate discussion: should we wait until 8 PM as our bulletin stated or should we start the service immediately? As we tried to decide what to do, we heard the Japanese planes coming. We ran into our trenches for protection. The Japanese dropped anti-personnel bombs, but we were safe in the trenches. I was so angry at the Japanese that I fired my machine gun at an overhead plane.

When the war ended in Europe on May 9, 1945, everyone celebrated V-E Day. We, who were fighting the war on the other side of the world, hoped that the European generals would remember that we were still AT WAR. When we entered the Mess Hall for dinner daily, we would ask the waiter, "Shorty, what do we have for dinner tonight?" He always answered, "CHICKEN-LICE".

V-J Day was on August 15, 1945 and we celebrated in whatever way we could. The Chinese people always have a festival on DOUBLE-TEN Day because it was on the 10th day of the 10th month (October 10) in 1914 that China became a republic. Special Services arranged a dance with girls that they brought from a women's college in Chengtu. Music was from a record player and 78 RPM records that we had. It was difficult to dance with the Chinese girls, but we all were happy that the war was over.

When WWII ended, our one thought was: when do we go home? The Army devised a plan where every soldier received points based on how long he was overseas, if he was in an area of combat, and whether he was wounded in enemy action. With the points we had, our group received orders in November, 1945 to return to the US. We flew over the hump to Calcutta in a B-24, a bomber that had been modified so it could carry passengers. In Calcutta, they gave us flu shots to prepare us for reaching the states in wintry December. That night, we were all sneezing and coughing from the flu shot.

We boarded the ADOLPHUS W. GREELEY, a troop ship that could accommodate 3,000 soldiers. They assigned me to guard duty which meant standing four hours in one spot, at the top of a ladder, ready to report anything that was wrong. I didn't care for that task at all and I asked if there were any other assignments. They changed my job and put me in the galley to work on the vegetable detail. Our route was: West across the Indian Ocean, North through the Arabian Sea and through the Suez Canal, Mediterranean Sea, and Atlantic Ocean to New York City. On November 22, 1945, my 24th birthday, the ship went through the Suez Canal. One of my tasks that day was to peel 50 pounds of onions. Because they announced through the P.A. system that we were in the Suez Canal, I'd dash up to the top deck, look to the left, and look to the right to view the scenery. The Mediterranean Sea was smooth but the Atlantic was rough and several men had to stay in the sick bay because of severe seasickness.

From New York City, we went by troop train to Seymour Johnson Field, for discharge. There was much paper work involved in being discharged and rather than do nothing, I volunteered to be a driver in the motor pool. For a week, I drove jeeps and trucks to different parts of the air base. On January 3, 1946, I was discharged, received my official papers, accumulated salary, and freedom.

CHAPTER 4

After The War

Since Ruth and I had been engaged for five years, we arranged to be married as soon as possible after my discharge from the army. We were able to obtain a catering hall, the President Chateau, at the corner of President Street and Utica Avenue, in Brooklyn. We invited as many of our family and friends as possible and the ceremony was performed on February 17, 1946 by Rabbi Maxwell Silver, the father of Marion Silver, one of Ruth's friends. We spent our honeymoon in New York City at a hotel on W. 45th Street, just off Times Square.

Fortunately, I was able to obtain a position at Midwood High School in Brooklyn, teaching Latin. I was a substitute teacher and took the place of the regular teacher who was on sabbatical leave for one semester. There were no openings for permanent teachers at the high school level and I went from school to school to fill temporary vacancies. I taught Latin at Curtis H.S., Staten Island, and at Newtown, HS, Elmhurst, L I.

The Board of Examiners said that the only examination they gave for regular teachers was to be a teacher of common branches in elementary schools. I decided to prepare for that examination because the Feinberg Law was passed in 1947, creating equal salaries at all levels. To study for that examination, I had to take additional Education courses at the elementary school level. Part of this test was English vocabulary, spelling, and grammar and I did well in those areas. My mother was a graduate of Washington Irving HS in Manhattan and she was very proficient in word meanings. She liked to read and whenever she came across a word that she did not know, she wrote it in a little notebook. When she had time, she would use a dictionary to look for the meanings of these words. She wrote on the cover of this notebook, SHER'S DICTIO-NARY, and from time to time, she would test me on the defini-tions of these tricky words. My mother, SARAH MANESSE SHER, was of great help to me with her word knowledge, and it was a very sad day in May 1947 when she died of heart failure. She was buried in Beth David Cemetery, Elmont, LI, in the plot of the Louis Heyman Friendship League. She encouraged me to have a sense of humor and use it in my working with children. Her persistence in supporting this "sense of humor" did have a result in my teach-ing and in my life as a whole. Many times when I was in charge of a meeting, I'd tell a story or anecdote to entertain the audience or to reinforce a point I wanted to stress.

In the summer of 1946, I taught Latin at Jamaica High School. The students were serious and I enjoyed helping them in work where they had been deficient. School started in the Fall of 1946 and I was so disappointed in not finding a teacher opening that I thought of looking for a job in the import-export business where I could use my knowledge of Spanish. I went to buildings in downtown Manhattan, going from office to office, asking if they needed a man who knew Spanish. This was discouraging and one day, I had a telephone call from Newtown, HS in Elmhurst, LI, that they needed a substitute teacher for three classes of Latin and two classes of Civics. I wasn't happy with the classes in Civics but teaching Latin made that semester worth while.

In the spring of 1947, I was assigned to Bushwick HS, Brooklyn. I stayed there for three semesters, teaching Latin, be-ginning French, and elementary Spanish. To earn extra money, I taught Latin at Curtis Summer HS in Staten Island in 1947. Be-cause it was hot, we kept the windows open and I could see what was going on in the New York Harbor. As I walked around the room, checking the work of the students, I would wave to the Queen Mary, the Normandy, or other large ships that were en route.

May 9, 1948 was a day of coincidence. It was a Sunday, it was Mother's Day, and my wife Ruth, became a mother. On that day, she gave birth to a son, whom we named STEVEN EDWARD SHER. He was born at the Long Island College Hospital in downtown Brooklyn. He was a big baby and was adored by his grandmother, BERTHA STEINER, and his grandfather, MORRIS SHER. In those days, a mother stayed in the hospital for one week after having her baby. Ruth was discharged on Sunday, May 15, and therein a problem was created. When Ruth left the hospital and walked down the steps to a taxicab, WHO WAS GOING TO HOLD THE BABY? Grandma, Grandpa, Ruth or I? The problem was solved by a practical nurse whom we had hired for a week to help us learn the routine of caring for a new baby. The nurse didn't ask any questions-she took Steve, wrapped him in a blanket, put a hat on his head, and carried him into the taxicab.

We lived in a two-room basement apartment of a brownstone house at 118 Fort Greene Place, Brooklyn, just one and a half blocks from the Brooklyn Academy of Music. We put Steve's crib in the kitchen and Ruth and I used the other room as a living room/bedroom. The daybed was a sofa during the day and opened into a double bed at night. We obtained a cot for the nurse and she slept on it in the kitchen, next to Steve's crib. She showed us how to wash the bottles for Steve's milk and how to prepare the formula, how to entertain him, how to change the diapers, and how to give him a bath. I was delighted with our healthy, fast-growing son and I gave out cigars and boxes of chocolates to the people at Bushwick HS, where I was teaching.

Since elementary schools went from kindergarten through grade 8, I was able to find a position in the fall term of 1948, at Junior HS 83, Manhattan. My class was an 8th grade Adjustment Class and I used this experience in meeting the requirements for the elementary school license. This junior high school was an all boys school and since my class was made up of boys from Puerto Rico, I had to teach them English, Arithmetic, and Social Studies. Since I had to help them make an adjustment to life in N.Y.C., I took them on trips to parks, museums, and places of interest. The boys were all poor and I helped financially by obtaining free transportation on the subways, els, and the ferry to Staten Island. They became accustomed to the routine and would often ask me, "Hey teach! When we go on a TREEP?" It was a difficult teaching job made even harder by transportation to the school. From Laurelton, LI, where we lived, to Jr. HS 83, I had to take the Q-5 bus to the subway, the E train to Lexington Avenue, and the Third Avenue El to 103rd Street, a total of 1 1/2 hours each way.

A Full Day in the Summer of 1948.

Although I had passed the examination to become an elementary school teacher, I still had to take special courses in elementary education to meet all of the requirements. The education courses I had taken at Brooklyn College were all at the secondary level and at the elementary level, I took: Principles of Education in the Elementary School; Teaching Art in the Elementary School; Teaching Music in the Elementary School; Techniques of Folk and Square Dancing; Science in a Program of Elementary Education; Handcrafts; Wood crafts; Psychology of Early Childhood.

Since I was teaching full time, I took these courses in the afternoons, evenings, and on Saturdays. In the Summer of 1948, I was able to meet these requirements in the following manner:

> 9 AM-1 PM: Teaching Latin at Curtis, HS, Staten Island
> 2 PM-3 PM: Taking the course Handcrafts at New York University School of Education at Washington Square, Manhattan
> 3 PM-4 PM: Taking the course Woodcrafts at N. Y. U. School of Education
> 4 PM-5:30 PM: I would take the subway to our apartment, play with Steve for a little bit, give him a bath, and give him a bottle of milk for his supper;
> 5:30 to 6 PM: I would eat my supper
> 7 PM-10 PM: I would take the subway to Brooklyn College, Flatbush, and then take a course in Psychology of Early Childhood.

When the courses that I took in the Summer of 1948 ended, Ruth and I looked for a house on Long Island. Ruth's mother, Bertha Steiner, came from her apartment at 1417 Avenue K to be the babysitter for Steve. We took the subway to 168th Street, Jamaica, and went to real estate agencies looking for a house that we liked and that we could afford. I was on Step 1 of the educational ladder and earned only $2, 700 per year. An agent showed us a two-story house at 137-37 234 th Street in Laurelton, L.I., that had three rooms downstairs and a finished basement, and three bedrooms upstairs. The house had been converted to a two-family dwelling and had a Certificate of Occupancy to verify the required alterations. Mrs. LAUB, the tenant, paid us $48 a month for rent and we were able to attain a G I mortgage at 4% through the Reliance Federal Savings and Loan Association, Jamaica. With my salary and her rent, we were able to pay off the mortgage in 20 years. Steve had a bedroom for himself, and Ruth and I slept on a daybed that we kept in the study. In 1951, when Dory was born, we asked Mrs. Laub to leave. She did and we all used the upstairs bedrooms.

In the Fall of 1948, I taught at Jr. H.S. 83 and in the evening , I went to NYU School of Education to take a course in 'Techniques of Folk and Square Dancing'. This was the equivalent of a course in physical education. For one hour, the instructor taught folk dance steps and how to do square dances. In the second hour, he allowed the students to call a square dance. Since we had done square dances at the Student Union Building in Lincoln, Nebraska, I was able to follow the instructor at NYU easily. I felt so confident in calling that I volunteered to call the dance, "Head Two Ladies Cross Over". There were 100 students in the class, they all followed my instructions, and all danced smoothly to the music, a record I had brought to class. The instructor complimented me for my performance and two weeks later, he told me that a group had called him, asking him to recommend a square dance caller. I was flattered by his offer and told him I would do this on the Saturday night they requested, at the Renaissance Casino in Harlem, at 142nd Street and Seventh Avenue. My wife, Ruth, could

33

play the piano and she played several songs: Oh Susanna, Red River Valley, Billy Boy, and other square dance tunes. It worked out very well and this became the first time I earned money as a square dance caller.

CHAPTER 5

A Regular Teacher in Elementary School

On February 10, 1949, I was appointed as a regular teacher and assigned to a full time position at P.S. 136 in St. Albans, Queens. Joseph MANDINA was the principal and he regarded me in a special light: there were 30 teachers on the faculty, and I was the only male teacher. He had a fifth grade class that was difficult to handle. In the Fall of the 1948 term, the class had four different teachers. What made it so troublesome? The class was large with a register of 41 and in that classroom, there were only 40 desks, screwed to the floor and immovable. When I arrived, one boy, ROBERT HILT was on the suspense register. He had been in the hospital for three weeks because of surgery for appendicitis. Consequently, all 40 students had a desk at that time. I learned the names of the pupils as quickly as I could but one day, there was a new student entering the room. The new face belonged to ROBERT HILT, mentioned a moment ago, and he sat in a different seat each day when someone was absent. If we had 100% in attendance, "HILTIE" had to share a seat with someone, causing two boys to use the same desk. At that time, we bought a new 1948 Plymouth (for $1,800) and I used it to drive from home in Laurelton to school in St. Albans.

Our house had 6 rooms and a finished basement and it was easy to make friends in the community. There were three Jewish

35

congregations in Laurelton, two conservative and one orthodox, and we had discussions about forming a Jewish congregation that was Reform. Other Jewish couples became interested
in this project and we concluded by forming the Free Synagogue
of Laurelton. We found a vacant store in Springfield Gardens
and converted it so we had a sanctuary for services and classrooms for the Sunday School. More families joined us and we
looked for land in Laurelton where we could put up a new
building. We found a piece of property on 233rd Street, just
north of Merrick Blvd. and organized a building campaign.
Some people thought that the words "Free Synagogue" meant
'without charge'. We knew that it meant "free thinking" and to
eliminate the misconception, we changed our name to Temple
Beth El. We hired a contractor and with the money in our Building Fund, we had him build the basement portion of our new
building. This was big enough to have a large central area for
our services and accordion-type doors which could create areas that became class rooms for our religious school. As our
membership increased, our activities grew and we were able to
have a Brotherhood, a Sisterhood, a Youth Group, a troop of
Boy Scouts, and a troup of Girl Scouts. I was quite active in the
affairs of Temple Beth El and in 1965, I became the President
for two years.

Our daughter, Dorothy, was born August 25th, 1951 and
we asked our tenants to move. They did, and we were able to
have the three bedrooms on the second floor: for Steve, for
Dorothy, and for Ruth and myself. In order to earn extra money
to make up for the rent that we no longer had from our tenants,
I taught in summer schools and made money as a square dance
caller. In 1950, I bought a CALIFONE record player and P.A.
System and used it to teach folk and square dancing as a recreational activity, and to call square dances for PTA's, church
groups, Legion Halls, and youth groups. The first dance I led
was on March 1952. It was for the Galahads, a group of teen-

agers who had a dance at a church in Springfield Gardens, L.I. My fee was $10.00.

In the evenings, I taught square dancing to adults in the gymnasium of Andrew Jackson High School and I taught folk dancing to adults at Public School 156 in Queens and at Junior High School 59. In 1950, I was elected into the Long Island Square Dance Caller's Association. This was especially helpful as I became friendly, personally and professionally, with other square dance callers.

One Saturday evening, I was calling for a square dance at an American Legion hall in Merrick, Long Island. It was a drinking crowd and they kept after me, "Have a drink?" I took a glass of ginger ale, put it near my record player, and nobody bothered me. Nobody knew that my glass had no liquor. In addition to calling square dances on Long Island, I ran dances in MAMARONECK, NY, PORT JERVIS, NY and GREAT BARRINGTON, MA. These dances that I ran on the evenings and weekends brought in money to supplement what I was earning as a beginning teacher.

New York State wanted to help WW II Veterans obtain a college education and the State offered scholarships to veterans who wanted to go to college. Since I had a B.A. from Brooklyn College and an M.A. from the University of Nebraska, I decided to enroll for a doctorate at Columbia University. After reviewing the requirements for a PhD or an Ed. D., I registered for the Doctor of Education degree. Columbia offered week day courses for teachers in the late afternoons and evenings and all day on Saturdays. I saw that I'd be able to teach at PS 136 until 3 PM and then drive to Manhattan to take courses at the Morningside Heights campus of Columbia. The area in which I was going to major was folk and square dancing in the elementary schools. As a teacher, I had to include Social Studies among the required subjects and I felt that children could learn folk dancing by correlating it with the areas that the Social Studies covered in Grades K – 6. My advisor at Teachers' College was

Dr. Richard Kraus, a recognized leader in Recreation and Square Dancing. In addition to all of the required courses I had to take, I had to write a thesis. Ruth was an excellent typist and she said that she would type it if we bought a new business-type machine. We bought an Olympia electric typewriter and I am forever grateful to her for typing my 495 page thesis, "The Place of Folk and Square Dancing in Teaching the Social Studies". I started taking courses at Columbia in 1954 and I finished nine years later.

I received help from D.A.N.Y.E., the Doctorate Association of New York Educators. This group consisted of women and men who had their doctorate and people who were working on their degree. One of the mambers was Dr. Eugene MALESKA, the superintendent of schools of a district in Upper Manhattan. Dr. Maleska was skilled in Latin and had the reputation of being an excellent wordsmith. When a member of D.A.N.Y.E. received the degree, it was customary for the association to give him/her a laurel wreath and a poem created by Dr. Maleska. The poem contained classical references and the one that he wrote for me shows his remarkable ability.

5/24/63
To Dr. Sher

Let's raise a toast to Dr. Sher, O!
He's the toast of Brooklyn Borough.
When Allen was a little geezer,
He loved the tongue of Julius Caesar,
And so from early A.M. into P.M.
He carpe'd every single dream
And dreamed that it would be his lot
To teach amo, amas, amat.
But Latin in New York was dead
So he became a clerk instead
And then he found some tasks to do
While learning at Nebraska U.
To Uncle Sam he gave his youth,
And then gave in and married Ruth.

In New York highs he got his licks.
Then fled to P.S. 1-3-6.
For fourteen years he searched his soul –
With Latin gone, what was his goal?
Then suddenly he found the answers:
He'd teach the kiddies to be dancers,
Not rock-n-rolling. That was tripe,
He'd teach them all the folksy type:
The tarantella and the hora
And how things are in Glockamorra.
And so they polkaed and they spieled
They dos-a-doed, Virginia-Reeled
And promenaded round in pairs
Until they all emerged as squares.
As Allen watched them in the gym
Another thought occurred to him;
"I'll show my colleagues and my buddies
How dancing fits with social studies".
"With this", he said excitedly
"I'll go and get my Ed. D."
And that was just what Allen got.
Ave' to him – I kid you not.

My father and Ruth attended the graduation exercises on the campus of Columbia University when I received my Ed.D. in March 1963. This poem was read by Dr. Maleska during the Laurel Ceremony for new doctorates at a dinner meeting of D.A.N.Y.E. held May 24, 1963 at the Brass Rail Restaurant at 5th Avenue and 43rd Street in New York.

One of the most valuable courses I took was "Skills in Social Recreation", taught by Dick Kraus. Using a textbook that he had written with this title, we learned activities in the areas of games, group singing, dramatics, and folk and square dancing. I was able to use these ideas when people called me to lead birthday parties for children. I provided games, stunts, and dancing that kept children from 6 to 16 busy, happy and entertained. Parents were delighted to see me organize a party where the youngsters were engaged.

As I look back at what I did in the 1950's and 60's, I see that I was involved in many activities besides the 8 to 3 teaching. In 1955, Steve wanted to join the Cub Scouts. He was accepted into Cub Pack 226 and I joined as a member of the adult committee to help the Cubmaster. After one year on the committee, I became the Assistant Cubmaster and following that, I became the Cubmaster. Our pack had six dens, each led by a Den Mother. We had about 60 scouts that met weekly with their Den Mothers and we gathered once a month, on a Monday evening at 7:30pm, as a pack, at Temple Beth El. Since I was the Cubmaster, I planned programs where I told stories, led games, had the boys sing and do scout cheers. We gave awards to the boys who completed the requirements for badges and it was inspiring to see how pleased the scouts and their parents were with this kind of official recognition. We took the boys on trips and on one Sunday evening, we all went to Madison Square Garden to see the Rangers play in a hockey game.

Steve left the cub pack at age 11 and then joined Boy Scout Troop 226. This troop had a very effective scoutmaster who encouraged the boys to fulfill requirements for merit badges. At age 15, Steve received the NER TAMID award, after passing all of the requirements for that badge.

Since I was a fifth–grade teacher, I taught all of the required courses: Reading, Writing, Arithmetic, Social Studies, Science, Art, Music, and Physical Education. If it was possible, I planned trips so that the children could supplement what we learned in school. I took them to the Staten Island Zoo, to the Museum of Natural History, to the museum at Wall Street and Nassau Street, in Manhattan, and to the Wonder Bread factory in Jamaica to see how bread was made. At the end of the tour, Wonder Bread gave each student a loaf of bread as a souvenir. We also went in May, to Alley Pond Park, in Queens, to participate in the City's Maypole Dance.

Every Tuesday morning, we took part in a school savings

program that was sponsored by the East New York Savings Bank. The children received envelopes which served as deposit slips and they would insert the money and their passbooks in the envelopes. I would put all of these deposits in a large envelope and a representative of the bank collected them, took them to the bank, and returned them on Thursday with the new amount recorded in the passbooks. The students always looked at their passbooks to see if their deposits were entered correctly.

One boy, HERMAN REIS, wanted to see if he could withdraw money. I gave him a pink withdrawal slip and he filled it out, requesting five cents. He was satisfied when his passbook came back on Thursday with a nickel in it. I supported this activity because it was good for children to learn the habit of saving. As an incentive to do banking every Tuesday, the bank would take a picture of any class that had 100% in banking, eight times in a row. The bank gave every student and myself a copy of the picture. I have several of these pictures and they serve as excellent reminders of the girls and boys I have had over the years at P.S. 136.

When I started to teach at P.S. 136 in 1949, the community of St. Albans was an all-white middle class neighborhood and consequently, the school was an all-white school. The neighborhood east of St. Albans had many black families and those children went to P.S. 30, on Baisley Blvd. In 1953, some black families moved into our school area and some white people became nervous over the change. Real estate agents were anxious to sell homes and they encouraged whites to move out and blacks to move in. Some took part in a practice called "churning the neighborhood". These folks would call people on the phone to say, "Do you know that so-and-so sold their house to blacks?" They put flyers in people's mailboxes offering CASH FOR YOUR HOUSE. Agents would put large ads in the local newspapers and this resulted in a complete turnover of a community. St. Albans went to an all-black neighborhood and our school became an all-black school. I continued to teach fifth grade classes.

5-1 Class; Mr. Allen Sher, Teacher; Public School No. 136, Queens Photograph presented with the compliments of THE EAST NEW YORK SAVINGS BANK – May 1961

STANDING: l. to r. Tyrone Hodges, James Murph, Martin Brommer, Barry Griffiths, Stephen Tyler, Mitchell Gordon, Edward Laub, David Hill, Peter Kings, Winston Nosworthy, Phillip Mechlowitz, Donald Francis, Michael Jhin, Manuel Ruiz, Victor Williams. FIRST ROW: top to bottom. Raymond Monfiletto, Janet Hall, Yvonne Guzman, Marcia Guidoni. SECOND ROW: Howard Tillman, Sheila Huggins, Yvonne Lake, Christine Simpson, Geraldine Graczyk. THIRD ROW: Henry Halperin, Ellen Roberts, Blanche Molfino, Patrice Gaulle, Elane Gutterman. FOURTH ROW: David Rissmeyer, Diane Shelby, Rosalyn Johnson, Beverly Morris. FIFTH ROW: Larry Liebs, Martin Blattberg, Robert Hawley

CHAPTER 6

Life in Laurelton, Long Island

In September of 1954, I started work at the Afternoon Center of P.S. 136, in Queens, as a Recreation Leader, and did this for ten years. At 3 o'clock, when school ended, I went downstairs, took off my jacket, put on a sweater and put a whistle around my neck. When the weather was good, we'd supervise the children as they played outdoors on the school playground. In the winter, we went upstairs to the school gymnasium where the boys and girls played basketball, climbed a rope, used the chinning bar, and did exercises on the mats. This went from 3-5pm daily and I received a salary of $2.25 per hour or $4.50 for the two hour session. I enjoyed working in Recreation, supervising children at play.

When the weather was agreeable, the boys liked to play softball. I would be the pitcher for both sides and I'd try to lob the ball over the plate so the boys would hit it. One boy who came regularly to play softball was Leonard FASULLO. Lennie was 15 years old but he was mentally retarded and played well with boys who were younger than he. Lennie left P.S. 136 and had a job working in one of the stores in the neighborhood. About four years after Lennie left school, I stopped for gasoline at the gas station on Merrick Boulevard and 235th Street. In those days, an attendant filled the tank for you and when I pulled up to the pump, a young man came from the office and asked, "How many gallons?" When the tank was filled, he came to me at the driver's window. When he noticed who I was, he jumped up and down, shouting, "Mr. Sher, my old teacher!" After paying him for the gasoline, I took a chance and said, "Lennie, the turn signal arrow isn't working. Can you fix it?" He lay down on the front seat, looked under the dashboard, located the fuse, replaced it with a new fuse and it worked fine. It was a real pleasure to see Lennie doing well at his job.

At 5pm, when all children left, there was silence in the school and I often sat there for five minutes, just enjoying the quiet. It was very helpful to have the extra money of $22.50 per week.

In the summer of 1959, I did not work and we planned a vacation trip with the family, driving from Laurelton, Long Island to Disneyland, south of Los Angeles, CA. We had bought a new 1958 Rambler and we drove across the country with five people in the car: Ruth and I in the front seat, and Steve, Dory, and my father in the rear seat. Luggage for all five fit snugly in the car's trunk.

We stopped overnight in:

Allen, Steve and Dory in front of Andrews Hall, University of Nebraska, July 11, 1959

•Washington, PA: just south of Pittsburgh;
•Greenfield, IN: just south of Indianapolis;
•Springfield, IL: where we toured the house where Abraham Lincoln lived;
•Davenport, IA; Hannibal, MO: where we had a guided tour of the cave that Mark Twain described when Tom Sawyer and Becky got lost

and their candle burned out;

•St. Joseph, MO: where we went to services in a Reform Congregation on a Friday night;

•Lincoln, NE: for a tour of the University of Nebraska campus;

•Colorado Springs, CO: it was July, we were wearing shorts and light clothing. We were about to leave the motel to drive to the top of Pike's Peak when the manager of the motel asked where we were going. When I said, "To the top of Pike's Peak", he said, "You'll need warmer clothing. It's 14,000 feet high and there's snow on the ground up there". Taking his advice, we put on warmer clothing and when we reached the summit, the first thing we did was buy a hot chocolate for everybody. On the way down, we stopped at a pull-off and gave Steve and Dory a chance to throw snowballs in July;

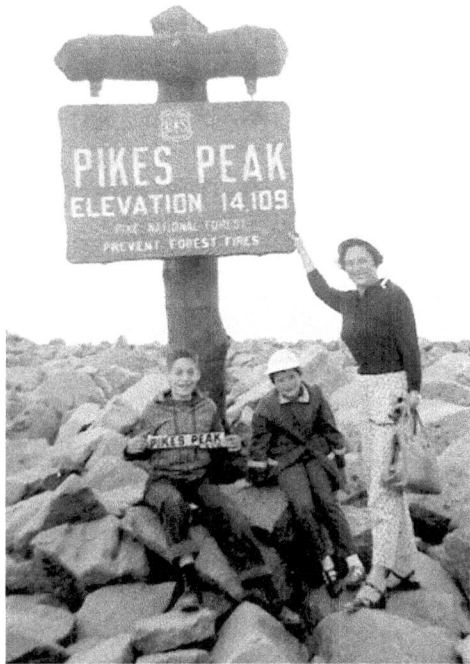

Ruth, Dory and Steve at Pike's Peak National Forest, Colorado Springs, CO, July 14, 1959

•Mesa Verde National Park, CO: we climbed into the cliff dwellings;

•Silverton, CO: we walked through a train of the DURANGO-SILVERTON narrow gauge railroad;

•Grand Canyon, AZ; -Zion National Park: in southwest Utah;

•Salt Lake City, UT: we toured the Mormon Tabernacle;

45

•Las Vegas, NV: Dad was the babysitter, and Ruth and I went into a casino. I played a penny slot machine, won some, lost some, and lost all of my $2.00.

•Long Beach, CA: while four of us went to Disneyland, Dad took a Pacific Electric interurban trolley to Los Angeles, where he visited with Aunt

Allen, Steve and Dory in front of the Denver & Rio Grande Narrow Gauge Railroad, Silverton Colorado, July 7, 1959

Ella and Uncle Julius. Dad flew home to Brooklyn and the four of us drove from Los Angeles north on the Mission Road to San Francisco. We went on the cable cars, had fun

Our faithful "Conestoga Wagon", the Rambler, going through the Tunnel Tree, Yosemite park, CA, August 4, 1959

at Fisherman's Wharf, drove down the twisting hill of Lombard Street, and north across the Golden Gate Bridge.

•Yosemite National Park, CA: a ranger told me about the park and as it grew dark, they made a fire high on a cliff above us. When the ranger called, "LET THE FIRE FALL", up above, they pushed the fire off the ledge and it descended in a RAIN OF FIRE.

•Ely, NV and Worland, WY;

46

•Mt. Rushmore, SD: we saw the heads of George Washington, Thomas Jefferson, Abraham Lincoln and Theodore Roosevelt, carved in granite by sculptor GUTZON BORGLUM;
•Chicago, IL: we visited with cousins Theodora and Dave SHAPIRO.

Riding the Hyde-Powell Street Cable Car, San Francisco, CA, August 1959

• • •

In 1961, the men of Laurelton formed a volunteer ambulance corps. At first, I thought we did not need an ambulance in our community. What made me change my mind was an accident on 137th Avenue, one block from where we lived. A teen-ager was driving his bicycle when he was hit by a car. People called the police and they sent a patrol car to the scene of the accident. They decided he should go to Queens General Hospital in Jamaica. It took about a half hour for the ambulance to come because the hospital was in Jamaica, a long distance from Laurelton. The injured boy had to lie at the side of the road until the ambulance

47

came and took him to the hospital.

We convinced ourselves that if we had an ambulance stationed in Laurelton, we could help people quickly when they needed medical treatment. I signed up as a member of the corps and took first-aid courses and training in how to drive an ambulance. We were ready to help people 24 hours a day and we did this by having two 12-hour shifts, from 6PM – 6AM and 6AM – 6PM. There were two men on each shift and we could do this because some men worked at night and some were able to the take the 6AM – 6PM shift.

We obtained a house on 223rd Street and used it as our headquarters. It had a two car garage and we kept our ambulances in the garage. When two men were on duty, they would go to our headquarters and check the ambulances to see that they were fully equipped and ready to roll when needed. When everything had been checked, we could go home, and if a call came for an ambulance, the telephone operator would call us at home. The two men on duty would meet at our headquarters and take one ambulance to the house where we were needed. I made myself available from 6pm – 6am on Mondays to Fridays and from 6am-6pm on Saturdays and Sundays. I went on 145 calls as a member of the Laurelton Volunteer Ambulance Corps and I always felt rewarded by knowing that I was helping others.

One of the men in the corps was a full-time employee of the Transit Authority. He was a motorman, and whenever I saw him, he had a little canvas bag which contained the controller handle and the brake handle that he used in operating the El trains. When he finished his schedule, he'd come home to Laurelton and make himself available as an ambulance driver. At age 65, he retired from the Transit Authority and knowing that I was a railroad fan, he gave me the two handles he used as a motorman. They are valuable to me and every so often, I hold the brake handle in my left hand, the controller in my right hand, and make believe I am driving a train.

One call came to me at home at 3AM. The telephone was right

next to our bed and when I was awakened by the ring, the operator said, "I have a call for you – a 16 year old boy has taken an overdose of sleeping pills and the doctor wants you to take him to the Emergency Room of the Long Island Jewish Hospital". I called my partner, dressed as quickly as possible, met my partner at the ambulance headquarters, and we drove to the boy's home. We had a folding chair in the ambulance and we took this into the house. We put the boy in the chair, strapped him in so that he wouldn't fall out, and carried him to the ambulance. I had him sit up even though he wanted to lie down and sleep. I sat with him while my partner drove as fast as possible to the hospital. I kept slapping the boy's face and I kept pinching his ear to keep him awake. "You're hurting me", he protested, but my only concern was to keep him from falling asleep. They were ready for him at the hospital and they used a stomach pump to remove the pills. My partner and I went home, happy that we had we had saved a life.

In August 1963, Ruth and I, together with Steve (age 15)

Allen at the controls of Car 303, Trolley Car Museum, Kennebunkport, Maine, with Dory, age 12 and Steve, age 15, August 1963

49

and Dory (age 12) drove on a vacation trip into New England and Canada. We visited Acadia National Park and then we went to Kennebunkport, Maine to tour the Seashore Trolley Museum. They have a private trolley right of way and we went for a ride on one of their trolleys. From Lubec, Maine, we crossed the bridge onto Campobello Island which is in New Brunswick, Canada. This was the summer home of President Franklin D. Roosevelt and his family often spent vacations there. In Canada, we traveled in Nova Scotia and New Brunswick. We did some shopping in Fredericton, just before we crossed back into Maine. All of us bought souvenirs of Canada and I bought two dozen gladiolus and tulip bulbs that I wanted to plant in our Laurelton garden. At the border crossing, the U.S. customs officer asked me how long we had been in Canada and where we had visited. I answered all of his questions and then he asked me to open the trunk of the car. He saw the paper bag containing the bulbs I had bought and without hesitation, he confiscated the bag, saying we were not allowed to carry bulbs into the U.S. from Canada. I tried to argue with the officer but he was adamant and threw the bulbs into a can of trash. I was very sad as I saw the bulbs, for which I had paid .75 go into a garbage can.

One of the saddest days I ever had was November 22, 1963. It happened to be the day of my 42nd birthday and it also was the day when our President, John Kennedy, was killed by an assassin in Dallas, TX. I heard the news on a Friday afternoon at P.S. 136 at 2:45pm, as we were ending our day's work. A neighboring teacher came over to me and whispered, "President Kennedy's dead. Someone shot at him in Texas". The news spread through school like wildfire, and while I usually stayed after 3 o'clock to do some school work, this time I hurried home and turned on the television. Every station carried the news of this disaster and tears came to my eyes as I thought of the problem it would cause. I was scheduled to run a square dance that evening for an American Legion post in Rosedale and I said to myself, ' How can I entertain people with this calamity touching us?' I went to the phone to tell the commander that I couldn't run the dance for them. As I reached for the phone, the telephone rang. It was a call from a representative of the Legion Post calling to say that they were cancelling their dance.

After teaching at P.S. 136 for fifteen years, I was able to transfer in June 1964 to P.S. 187, at 63rd Drive and Marathon Parkway in Little Neck, Long Island. That summer, Steve and Dory went to a summer camp in New Jersey, and Ruth and I went on a cruise to the West Indies. We left from New York City and visited St. Thomas, Puerto Rico, Barbados, Martinique, and Bermuda. We were seated at the Captain's Table because I was listed as Dr. Allen Sher.

When Steve was a teenager, he had a lot of trouble with his hands. Doctors said his sweat glands were dysfunctional and he developed blisters that were so severe that he couldn't play ball and couldn't even hold a pen. We heard of a skin clinic at Bellevue Hospital in Manhattan where they prescribed a cream that helped him. One day, I took him to Bellevue, driving from Laurelton to East New York where we could take the 14th Street Canarsie Line into Manhattan. On Linden Boulevard and Rockaway Avenue, we stopped at Coney Island Joe for a hot dog sandwich that Steve liked. Joe's specialty was two long frankfurters on French bread with onions and sauerkraut, and it cost 25 cents.

In 1965 and 1966, I served as President of Temple Beth El. Our congregation had been growing in membership and the Board of Trustees voted to construct a new building to go on top of the basement structure already present. We had a building campaign and we were aided by professional advisors to assist us in raising $500,000. Some valuable advice was, "Don't ask anyone to donate $500. Ask for $100 a year for five years." With the help of our Building Committee, we were successful and hired the WILLIAM ISER Construction Company to be the contractors. The Ridgewood Savings Bank promised a permanent mortgage and the Meadow Brook National bank gave us a building loan of $485,000. This was the biggest check I ever

The Trustees and Officers of the Congregation pledged to guarantee the mortgage payments. Accepting this faith, the Ridgewood Savings Bank promised a permanent mortgage and the Meadow Brook National Bank promised a building loan. Construction started in March 1966, and proceeded through that summer. The sanctuary and offices were built on the new property and the social hall was constructed on top of the old reinforced building. Large permanent classrooms were made to replace the crowded temporary rooms that had served the religious school so faithfully.

Dr. Allen Sher

High Holiday Services in September of 1966 were held in the new sanctuary. There were no windows, no doors, and no heat. There was only a bare concrete floor and it rained — but, . . . we were in our new building and we persevered. The following year showed the completion and the decoration of the interior.

The new Temple Beth El of Laurelton has taken its place as an outstanding addition to the community. The Queens Chamber of Commerce, moreover, has taken note of the beauty of the structure, selecting it as a prizeworthy religious building. On December 5, 1967, this significant organization awarded a plaque to Lou Stone, the President of the Congregation, for excellence of design and civic value. Many civic and religious events have already taken place in the new Temple Beth El. The Congregation has been, is, and will continue to take an active part in community affairs. It will continue to take a keen interest in the spiritual and secular needs of the children, teenagers, adults, and senior citizens of Laurelton.

DR. ALLEN SHER

had and I turned it over to Bill Iser so he could begin work.

When enough additions were made, we were ready to put the cornerstone in place. Where do you go for a cornerstone? We knew a man with a business near Beth David Cemetery in Elmont, Long Island, where he sold cemetery monuments. We asked him if he would donate a piece of granite we could use as a cornerstone. He agreed and even put the lettering on the stone for us. When it was ready, he phoned to say that the work was done and we could call for it. Who will go for the cornerstone? The president, of course. The workers put it into the trunk of my '62 Rambler. The stone weighed over 400 lbs. and was so heavy that I thought the rear of the car would go down and the front would be pointed towards heaven. I reached the Temple without any problem and men from the Iser Company removed it from the trunk. Congressman Joseph ADDABO, of Ozone Park, was present for the cornerstone ceremony on Sunday, April 24th, 1966. One year and eight months later, on Friday, December 15, 1967, Rabbi Dr. Maurice EISENDRATH, President of the Union of American Hebrew Congregations, delivered the Sermon of Dedication.

The new Temple Beth El took it's place as an outstanding addition to the community. The Queens Chamber of Commerce, moreover, chose our building as praiseworthy religious building and presented a plaque for excellence of design and civic value.

Because I was a teacher at P.S. 187 in Little Neck, Long Island, I was able to drive to school easily, using the Belt Parkway. As my years of experience increased, so did my salary. I found that I had more time at home, doing chores around the house and spending more time with the family.

CHAPTER 7

Vermont, the
Green Mountain State

Our son, Steve, went to Brooklyn College from 1965 to 1969, majoring in Urban Planning. We had two cars in the family and we let Steve use one of them to drive to college. After graduation, he went to Cornell University. He continued to study REGIONAL PLANNING and received his Master's Degree in 1971.

In October of 1968, the teachers of New York City went on strike for two weeks, protesting to the Mayor and the Board of Education that we did not want our schools to be run by the communities in which the schools were located. We felt that this would weaken the school system and would create favoritism in the appointing of teachers. We were not paid for these two weeks and this shortage of income affected the teachers and their families. As we approached Christmas, I went to the Post Office to see if I could get a job as a temporary worker to help with the Christmas mail. I applied for a job on the 4P.M. – midnight shift and was hired to work at the post office in Flushing, sorting mail and handling packages. I taught until 3 P.M., drove to the Flushing post office, and worked until midnight. When all of our mail was distributed, I drove home, slept five hours, did lesson plans for my class and was at P.S. 187 by 8:30 A.M.

While Steve was at college, he met ANITA SCHILLER, a major in Elementary Education. They went together for three years and were married on January 16, 1971, at Temple Beth Shalom in

Flatbush by Rabbi MILLSTEIN. It was hard to find a job in Urban Planning in the New York City area and he went to Washington, D.C., for employment. He worked on the D.C. Zoning Commission for eleven years, and became the Secretary, one of the top men on the Commission. Steve was in charge of 13 people and came in contact with many lawyers and congressmen. The attorneys he worked with saw how skilled he was in zoning and corporate affairs, and hired him to work as their Zoning Consultant. Steve and Anita bought a house in North Potomac, MD, and have lived there for about 35 years.

Our daughter, Dory, went to Queens College from 1969 to 1971 and married Philip EHRLICH in July 1971. They wanted to be married at sunrise, at the top of Bear Mountain, NY. We convinced them that such a place and time were inconvenient and they agreed to be married locally by Rabbi MILLSTEIN of Temple Beth El of Laurelton. They wanted to have an outdoor wedding and we were able to arrange it in Brookville Park, in Rosedale, Long Island on a Sunday at 1:00PM. After the ceremony, we all adjourned to the synagogue for the reception. There was one difficulty in having the ceremony in Brookville Park: the Park was directly in line with airplanes that were landing at Kennedy Airport. In fact, the planes were only about 100 feet high as they zoomed to the airport on their approach to land. They were very, very loud and so noisy that you couldn't hear people talk when the planes were overhead. I called the Control Tower at the airport and asked if they would have the planes land in a different direction for the hour that we would be in the park for the wedding. They agreed to my request and with no planes overhead, we had a quiet and proper wedding.

With both of our children married and not in New York City any longer, Ruth and I decided it was time to move as well. Many people from the north were moving to Florida or to the southwest to places like Arizona or New Mexico. We were different, however, and we chose to move to Vermont. We had been to the Green Mountain State for short vacation trips and we liked the scenery, the places of interest, the people and the weather. The population of Vermont is about 600,000 and is so small that it is next to Wyoming as being lowest in population in the U.S. Some people claim that Vermont has more cows than people! The first half of October in southern Vermont is a beautiful time and place in the United States. The sugar maple trees along every country lane burst out in scarlet and gold and the autumn sun brightens the white church steeples.

The largest city in Vermont is Burlington, but we chose to live in Rutland, which is the second largest. We found a very attractive ranch-style home, with five rooms and a finished basement: there was a large country kitchen that had a wood burning fireplace, a living room, and three bedrooms. Ruth was able to use one room for her books and painting studio. I had one room for my books, desk, and file cabinets, and the last was our bedroom. All rooms had windows where we saw green grass, green bushes, trees and the Green Mountains.

On Friday, June 30, 1972, the last day of school, we moved from Laurelton to our new home at 62 Meadowbrook Road. We had several months to prepare for the move and we packed our belongings in 151 cardboard cartons. Many were sturdy boxes (that had previously contained liquor bottles) and I put a number on each box. In a notebook, I listed what the box contained and when the movers unpacked the vans, we could tell the men into what rooms they should put each box.

On Sunday, July 2nd, our next door neighbors, Sarah and Frank MAINOLFI had a block party in their backyard to welcome us. We appreciated their efforts and it was a marvelous way for us to meet the people of our new neighborhood. On Monday, July 3rd, Ruth was making breakfast when all of a sudden, we had no electricity. Ruth thought she had caused trouble using the electric stove. In Laurelton and in Brooklyn, we had always used gas stoves. She figured she had erred somewhere with the dials of the electric stove and that had caused a short circuit. I went outside and saw the Mainolfis and the Sullivans puzzling over the outage. Nobody had a satisfactory explanation but the power company came and their workers found the answer: a squirrel scampering from pole to pole on one of the wires that carries the electricity had run into a transformer. This was too powerful for the squirrel and it died, causing the short circuit. Electricity was restored and we never had that kind of trouble again.

The next day was the fourth of July and we drove to Plymouth, VT to attend the opening of the Calvin Coolidge Museum. Calvin Coolidge was born in Plymouth and a museum had been built to contain information about him, his family, and his Presidency. Plymouth is a modest mountain hamlet where the unpretentious president was born and is buried. On July 4, 1972, there were speeches and music to go with the ceremony, but the outstanding attraction to Ruth and me was a performance by the Ed Larkin Contra Dancers, right out on the Plymouth Village green. We knew folk dancing and square dancing, and had done some contra dancing in New York. The Larkin Group's dancing, in old-time costumes, accompanied with music by a three piece band, made such a presentation of Portland Fancy, Petronella, Honest John, and Hull's Victory that I asked Ray Hull, the leader, if there were outsiders that sometimes danced with their group. Ray told us that they were busy performing all over Vermont during the summer and autumn, but they did have open houses once a month, on Saturday nights, in East Bethel, VT, during the winter and spring months. We had told him that we'd like to come to an open house to learn their dances, and he said we'd be welcome.

In Rutland, there was a center for senior citizens and Ruth and I visited it often. There were classes, rooms for square dancing, and facilities for games of all kinds. One class was painting of figurines and it was one that Ruth took. The instructor was very helpful and she gave Ruth enough of a foundation that when the class ended, Ruth wanted to continue painting on her own at home. She bought an easel, paint brushes of all sizes, and whatever she needed for oil paintings. There was no trouble about what to paint

Ruth's Painting of Covered Bridge

because all she had to do was look through our windows to see trees and mountains. With her camera, she took pictures in color and used the prints as subjects for her paintings. At times that we were traveling to other parts of Vermont, Ruth would carry her camera and take pictures of scenery that appealed to her. We were traveling to Chelsea, VT one afternoon when she suddenly shouted, "Stop the car!" I thought we had hit something or there was some kind of trouble. Explanation? We had passed a covered bridge and she wanted to take a picture of it. We were on a narrow two-lane country road and it wasn't easy to back up to this bridge. I did, and Ruth took a picture of the bridge and did a painting of this covered bridge over the White River near Tunbridge. It is so colorful and realistic that I have it right now on a wall of my living room.

In October, many tourists come to Vermont to see the maple trees with their changing colors. On Columbus Day, October 12th, Rutland had an Art in the Park display at the corner of US 7 and US 4. These highways were used by motorists who wanted to see the Green Mountain State, and many would stop to look at the art work. Artists who wanted to sell their paintings were permitted

59

to display their work on the grass of the park and on several of these Columbus Day exhibits, Ruth and I were there displaying and helping to sell her paintings. She was successful and sold some of her art work each year.

Trains and trolley cars have been a life-long interest of mine. My parents never had an automobile, and if we traveled anywhere in New York City, we took a train, trolley car, or bus. Fare was just 5 cents and transfers from one line to another were free. When I went by subway or elevated lines, nothing pleased me more than to stand at the front of the first car. I loved to see that the motorman of our train obeyed the green, yellow, and red signal lights and that he pressed the proper buttons when we had to switch tracks. In the summer, on some lines, they would open the front end door of the first car and passengers would have cool air come in as the train moved between stations.

As an adult, I joined the Electric Railroaders' Association and the Railroad Enthusiasts. The ERA had programs about trains and trolley cars that ran by electricity, while the RR enthusiasts dealt with long distance trains that ran by coal and steam, and later, by diesel power. I also belonged to the Trolley Museum in East Haven, CT, and went there to look at the trolleys and to ride on the 1 mile track that the members of the museum maintained. Early in July 1972, the president of the Trolley Museum appealed to us for help.

The museum was open seven days a week and even on weekends; there were enough volunteers for all of the tasks but it was hard to run the cars on weekdays because so many men were working at their regular jobs. I answered the appeal of our president and agreed to volunteer on one weekday from 10 AM – 5 PM, when the museum was open. On July 24, 1972, I drove from Rutland to East Haven, Ct and served as conductor on an open-air trolley. I walked along the running board from one end of the car to the other, punching the tickets of the passengers. At the end of the line, we had to reverse ends. The motorman took his control keys to the other end of the car and

Allen at the controls of a trolley, Branford Trolley Museum
July 24, 1972

I changed the poles, lowering the one at the front and raising the one at the rear so that the pole would touch the wire with the electricity.

The last ride for passengers was at 5 PM. The motorman was then supposed to take the car into the barn but he asked me if I wanted to operate the car for one trip. He explained what I had to do with the key, the controller, and the brake. I drove the car to the end of the line and I changed to the other end of the car while the motorman reversed the poles. I left the museum that day at 6 o'clock and returned home to Rutland by 10 PM. I was very, very pleased with my day's "work" and Ruth said she took one look at my face and knew that it had been a successful day.

As we continued to reside in Vermont, I learned of trolley cars that had run in Rutland. Electric trolleys had begun to operate in 1894 but there were horse cars from 1885 – 1895. Service was extended to Castleton, Lake Bomoseen and Fair Haven, and there were 26 electric cars in operation. From conversations that I had with Richard Ryan and others from Rutland who knew about the trolleys, I wrote a monograph entitled, "The Street Railways of Rutland". It was published in the Winter of 1980 as the Quarterly of the Rutland Historical Society.

A railroad fan collects railroad items, and over the years, I

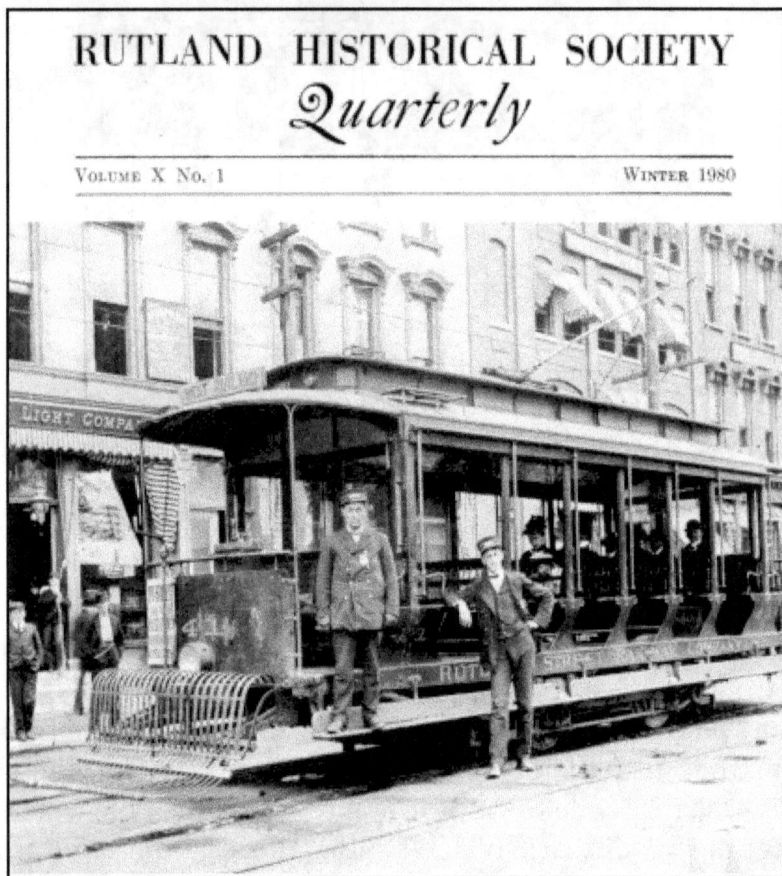

RUTLAND HISTORICAL SOCIETY
Quarterly

VOLUME X No. 1   WINTER 1980

have collected post cards, magazines, and books that deal with trains. In 1975, Ruth and I flew to Chicago to see Dory and her husband, Philip. We did some sightseeing and Ruth went shopping on Michigan Avenue – while I rode on the ELs and subways. I also went to the Merchandise Mart to the headquarters of the Chicago Transit Authority for some pamphlets about Chicago's trains. They had some items for sale, and one was a changemaker that conductors and bus drivers used when collecting fares. Now that they expect riders to have exact fare, the changemakers became surplus equipment. I bought one for $6.25 and it has the initials CTA engraved on it. I use it at home whenever I need coins and I think I'm a conductor whenever I click out some change. I have two conductor's caps, one with a badge from the New York City Transit Authority. The other is marked BRAKEMAN and is from the Norfolk and Western Railroad.

Ruth was excellent at secretarial work and obtained a job at Castleton College, working in the Office of the Registrar. She reviewed the records of juniors and seniors to make sure they had taken all the required courses for their majors. While she was secure with her position at Castleton, I was looking for something I could do in the Rutland area. It happened that the College of St. Joseph the Provider had an opening in the Education Department. After an interview with the college officials, I was hired as an Associate Professor, teaching courses in Education and Children's Literature. I have always been a happy teacher and even though the salary was low, I was glad to be in the field of Education, helping others to become teachers. I also taught courses in Early Childhood, a program which gave students the ability to work in day care centers. The State Department of Education in Montpelier asked me to lead a workshop in Folk Dancing and Singing Games for young children. I did this at the Holiday Inn in Rutland and there was good attendance.

At the invitation of Joe GIANCOLA, a well-known realtor and building contractor in Rutland, I joined the Board of Directors of the Sugar Maple Children's Center on North Main Street in Rutland. It served 400 children and was the biggest day care center in Vermont. Sugar Maple's hours were from 6:30 AM to 6:30 PM and it provided an educational environment for children aged 2 to 6. Parents of these children could leave their youngsters in a day care center that took such good care of the boys and girls that the mothers and fathers could work without worrying about their little ones.

As a way of encouraging parents to dance and play with their children, I led a family folk dance. This was on a Sunday afternoon, in the gymnasium of the Immaculate Heart of Mary School in Rutland. There was a good turnout for this dance and children and parents had a pleasant get-together.

Sugar Maple had a pond behind the building and the teachers took children on canoe rides, as one of the experiences they provided for the little ones. In the evening, they would leave the canoe on the grass and nobody ever bothered it. One morning, when they opened the day care center, they found that someone had stolen the canoe. Charlotte MUCH, Director of Sugar Maple, called me and asked, "Allen, can you get us another canoe?"

I went to the Rutland Public Library and consulted the Foundations Directory. I located a foundation that gave grants to institutions in New Jersey and in Vermont. I submitted a proposal of $400. for a new canoe, together with information about the Sugar Maple Children's Center. The foundation sent one of its members to Rutland to verify that the Center really needed the money. The agent was impressed by everything he saw and the foundation sent us a check for $400 to purchase a new canoe.

Between the main building of Sugar Maple and the pond, there was a level area where the girls and boys played outdoor games. One evening, when the Board of Directors was having its monthly meeting, Charlotte Much, the Director, asked Joe GIANCOLA if we could obtain a caboose that we could put in this open area. She felt that the children would learn what a caboose was, would use it for climbing up and down, and could use it for a library when we renovated the interior. Joe looked at me and said, "Can you get a caboose for us?" I said, "I'll try."

The Norfolk and Western Railroad had cabooses that they weren't using anymore and I took a chance and wrote to John FISHWICK, President of the N & W RR Company. I asked him if he would donate a caboose for the children of our day care center. He replied that they had no cabooses they could give to us but he suggested that I try the Delaware and Hudson Railway in Albany. Mr. Joseph WILSON of the D & H called me to say they could not donate a caboose but they would sell one to us. "How much for a

A caboose, put onto its tracks at the Sugar Maple Day Care Center Saturday afternoon, was put into place by Rutland Army Reserve Engineer Batallion 368, Company C. (Photo by Morrissey).

Follow-Ups
On News

Caboose Comes

The Leaf Patch Nursery on North Church Street was scheduled to open a new arts and crafts center on July 15. However, its appearance was delayed due to a strike by clerks on the Norfolk & Western Railway.

What does one have to do with the other? The new arts and crafts center is a Delaware & Hudson Railroad caboose, which the nursery obtained for $1 Saturday it arrived at the nursery.

A recent strike among clerks at the Norfolk & Western caused a backlog of train orders, forcing the caboose to sit on its tracks for a while until its turn to roll came up.

Engineers and Giancola Construction Co. transported the caboose to its permanent homestead on North Church Street.

The movers had devised a special route to pull the caboose through the city to avoid pulling down wires along the way.

That afternoon Kiwanis Club members tackled repairs to the caboose, scrubbing and painting it so that it will be ready for occupation by children early this week.

---

caboose?" I asked. Joe Wilson said, "One dollar." He sent me a bill of sale, I obtained a check for one dollar from the Sugar Maple Treasury and sent it to him in Albany. Mr. Wilson replied that the caboose was in Rouse's Point, New York, that he would attach it to a southbound freight train and that a train going to Rutland would leave it for us in the Rutland Freight Yards.

It was our responsibility to move it from the freight yards to the Sugar Maple Center. How do you move a caboose through the streets of Rutland? I called Captain David ZSIDO of the Rutland Army Reserve and he arranged for his men and equipment to move the caboose on Saturday, August 5, 1978. I had called Charlie BISCHOFF of the Vermont Railway Company in Rutland for a donation of two lengths of rail and twenty ties. Charlie gave us the rail and ties and Joe GIANCOLA and his men laid a concrete bed on which the ties and tracks were set as the home for the caboose.

David ZSIDO and his men of the Army Reserve met at the freight yards at 10AM with a crane and two low-bed trailers for the caboose and the wheels. The crane lifted the caboose, and put it on one trailer and the wheels on the other trailer. With a Rutland police car leading the parade, we moved slowly from the freight yards on South Street to West Street, up the hill to Main Street, and left on Main Street to the Sugar Maple Building. Joe GIANCOLA was there with his own crane. He lifted the wheels from the trailer and placed them on the rails. Then he lifted the caboose, set it down exactly on the wheels, and inserted the pins to lock it in place.

The Army Reserve, the Giancola Construction Company, the Police Department, and the Fire Department all worked together beautifully and the project took place without any accident or damage. Six men of the Rutland Kiwanis Club painted the caboose and it had a new look. The caboose is now in place and it will be a secure and lasting contribution to the children of Rutland. The Rutland Daily Herald, in the August 7, 1978 edition had an article and picture of the caboose as it was set in place.

Speaking of things that were stolen, Ruth and I had an unfortunate experience on February 10, 1973, on a Saturday night in East Bethel, VT. We had gone there to do contra dancing at an Open House of the Ed Larkin Contra Dances. It was 12 degrees below zero but there was no trouble driving in our 1972 Plymouth Valiant. Most of the forty people there were farmers who came from Central Vermont and were accustomed to going out in the snow and cold weather. Ray Hull was the prompter and started at 8PM, leading us in THE TEMPEST, THE CONNECTICUT RIVER CONTRA, and WARREN 'S HORNPIPE, stopping and explaining parts that we found difficult. About 10PM, Ray said, "Let's stop and have a little snack." We all went downstairs where the women sold ham sandwiches and egg salad sandwiches they had prepared (10 cents each) and doughnuts (5 cents) and coffee (5 cents). At 10:45PM, all went upstairs for another hour of contras. Ruth and I had really enjoyed the dancing and the sociability but we decided to head for home instead of returning for the last hour of dancing. We walked out to our car and I opened the door on Ruth's side. The ceiling light did not go on but I didn't worry because I knew that sometimes that light didn't work. I sat down behind the steering wheel, put the key into the ignition and turned the key to start the motor. Nothing happened. I tried again. There was no sound at all.

I went around to the front of the car, lifted the radiator hood, and saw that someone had stolen the battery! Our Plymouth looked new because it was only six months old and maybe somebody needed a battery. Ruth and I went back to the group and they were surprised to see us return. We told one of the men that someone had stolen our battery. The word went from one person to the next like wildfire, "Someone stole their battery!" They didn't know how to help us. One man had a friend about thirty miles from East Bethel who'd come down; someone else, nearby, had a battery in his garage. He trotted out, found the battery, installed it for us, and said, "Try it." The engine started and we thanked everyone for their concern. On the way home we stopped at a station of the Vermont Highway Police. It was 12:05AM by that time but an officer recorded the information about the theft. We reached home safely and on Monday, I reported this to our Allstate Insurance Agent. Allstate listened sympathetically, said we had been using the battery for five months, and sent me a check for $32.50 to buy a new battery.

At the next dance, I returned the used battery to the man who had given it to us. We never learned who had taken our battery but Ruth and I guessed that it may have been some poor person who needed it but didn't have money to pay for one. As we continued to dance with the Ed Larkin group, we learned many contra dances, progressive dances, and reels. We would practice these dances at our Open Houses in East Bethel, and then would dance them for the public at the Tunbridge Fair and whenever we had bookings in towns throughout the state.

The names of some of these dances were:

CHORUS JIG
EIGHT HAND REEL
FAIRFIELD FANCY
JEFFERSON'S REEL
LADY WALPOLE'S REEL
PETRONELLA
PORTLAND FANCY
RAMBLER'S HORNPIPE
TWIN SISTERS
WASHINGTON QUICKSTEP

The fireplace in our kitchen was one of the house's attractive features and we prepared to use it as soon as the cold weather arrived. We bought a cord of wood, stored it in the garage, and put a few chunks in a holder next to the fireplace. Late in October, we made a fire in the fireplace, expecting to enjoy its warmth and the glowing embers of the burning logs. Before the logs became embers, however, the kitchen filled with smoke. I never realized that the fireplace had a damper and that I had to open the damper to let the smoke go up the chimney!

One day we noticed big black ants crawling near the fireplace. We thought they might be termites and we anticipated a problem with the building. I took some of the ants to the agricultural office and they explained that they we were not termites – they were carpenter ants that had been in the chunks of wood and had come out because of the heat in the fireplace.

Experiences With the
Kiwanis Club of Rutland

In the Fall of 1973, Joe GIANCOLA invited me to join the KIWANIS Club of Rutland. This was an organization with which I was not familiar. I thought that Kiwanians were professional men: doctors, lawyers, storekeepers, and businessmen. They asked me, a teacher, to become a member and when I attended one of their meetings and met interesting men of Rutland of all ages and professions, I accepted the invitation. Their purpose was "to serve" and this meant children, handicapped adults, and senior citizens. We organized various fundraising projects and then we used the money to help poor people.

In April of 1974, the club announced that it would sponsor a Pancake Breakfast. One member had a motel on U.S. 4 in Mendon, a busy highway for people who wanted to ski on the slopes of Pico Peak and KILLINGTON MOUNTAIN. The motel had a dining room and our Kiwanis member let us use it for the occasion. They advertised: ALL YOU CAN EAT – juices, pancakes, eggs, bacon, sausage, biscuits, and beverages – for $2.50. We scheduled this for the Saturday and Sunday of the Palm Sunday weekend and we had many customers. In fact, we had so many customers that we were practically out of food on Saturday. We went to the A & P and bought more juice, pancake flour, eggs and coffee because the food was good and people were asking for seconds. I was the pancake flipper on Sunday and I worked without a pause from 6:30AM until 1:30 in the afternoon. Our net profit was a disappointing $150.00, one reason being that we had to pay over the counter prices for the Sunday food.

As I became involved in the activities of the Kiwanis Club, I was appointed the Chairman of the Youth Services Committee. We arranged activities for children and teen-agers: a fishing derby, horseback rides, and taking mentally handicapped teens to lunch.

Sue HATHAWAY was the leader of a 4-H Club of about 24 girls and boys. She was interested in horses and many of the activities of her group had to do with horses. Sue and I became friends because we were both on the Board of Directors of the Sugar Maple Children's Center. As a Kiwanis project, we arranged for physically handicapped youngsters to go on horseback rides. Sue provided 4-H members with their horses. We set up an oval near the College of St. Joseph and the Kiwanians lifted the children on and off the horses. The teen-agers walked the horses around the loop and we walked alongside to help the children stay in the saddles. We did the same thing for mentally handicapped adults. Here were people who had never been on a horse and making this possible became a service project for the 4-H'ers and for us.

We repeated this project again on the campus of the College of St. Joseph. We made steps out of cinder blocks and the men and women used the steps to climb up to reach the saddles. As with the children, our Kiwanis men were there to help the people into the saddles and we walked alongside the horses to help if needed. The men and women stood in line and one by one they approached the horses. One woman hesitated when it was her turn and she went to the end of the line. She did this twice and people began to tease her because she wouldn't go for a ride. We encouraged her, helped her go up the steps and we stayed with her until she sat in the saddle. She held the reins and when the 4-H leader was ready to walk the horse, the woman in the saddle began to cry. We helped her out of the saddle and onto the ground.

All I could think was, 'we tried to do something good and in one case, it didn't work'.

Another service project of our Kiwanis club was to take youngsters out to lunch. We arranged it on a Saturday morning when most men had the day off and were not working. The Brandon Training School had a Recreation Director and when I told him eight Kiwanians wanted to do this, he paired us off with eight boys. I spent the day with FRISBEE MORGAN. We met in the lounge and then the boys took us on a tour of their campus and dormitories. Just before noon, we drove to a diner on US 7 near Pittsford. When the waitress saw we were sixteen people, she pushed the tables together and the boys sat on one side and we sat opposite, facing them. The waitress gave each of us a menu and we looked to see what we wanted to order. I thought Frisbee might have trouble reading the menu so I told him what was on the card. I said, "Frankfurter" and Frisbee said, "I'll have it". I said, "Hamburger", and Frisbee said, "I'll have it". I read, "Cheeseburger" and Frisbee said, "I'll have it". We agreed on a hamburger and I told the waitress that's what we wanted. She jotted it down on her pad and I asked her if we could have an order of French fried potatoes while waiting. In a few minutes, she brought in a plate of the potatoes and put it on the table between Frisbee and me. I reached out, took one potato, and started to eat it. Frisbee said to me in a scolding tone, "Use your fork".

Other service projects of the Kiwanis club were:

- Square dances for people with handicaps and in wheelchairs;
- Cutting trees into firewood for the disadvantaged;
- Spelling contests against the Rotary Club;
- Blood donor contests among the service clubs of Rutland.

Rutland had several nursing homes and working with the recreation directors, we arranged square dances for people in wheelchairs. The men of our club would push the people in their wheelchairs according to the directions of the square dance caller. I was the caller and used singing calls like "Hinkey, Dinkey, Parlez

Vous, Head Two Ladies Cross Over, Sioux City Sue and Billy Boy". Since I had a record player and 78 RPM records, there was no problem with music for the dances. Before doing a dance with music, we'd have a walk-through so that the pushers knew what to do with their people. In a short time, all learned how to do calls like, "Forward and Back, Dosido, All Join Hands and Circle Left and Promenade". We did these square dances at the Eden Park, Beverly Manor, and McKerley Health Center Nursing Homes.

In 1980, we spent a Saturday in the Rutland City Forest, cutting down trees for firewood. A city forester had marked the trees that we should cut down. We did that, and then we sawed the trunks into twelve-inch lengths. We then split the logs into chunks. I had no experience in forestry but when chunks of wood were ready, I gathered them and tossed them into trucks we had brought. We started at 8:30 AM and it was 10 degrees below zero, but we were busy until 3:00 o'clock and didn't mind the cold weather. We donated half of the wood to people who needed it and sold the rest at $75 a cord.

At the College of St. Joseph, one of the Education courses I taught was "Language Arts in the Elementary School". We helped our students learn how to teach spelling and I always included Spelling Contests as a way of motivating children to improve in Spelling. Every year, at the end of May, there is a National Spelling Bee in Washington, D.C. and because it is televised, children and parents can watch the nation's best spellers participate in the competition. It always bothered me to see a child misspell a word and be led off stage to the Comfort Room. In this room, the children could give vent to their frustration. They could cry, they could kick or punch an inflated clown, they could tear paper into shreds, and they could kick balls with all their might. To reduce the unhappiness on the part of the youngsters, I created the idea of a Spelling Contest: children would be on a team and if they spelled a word correctly, they would score two points for their team. If they misspelled a word, they would receive no points but they were not eliminated – they would remain in the contest. This worked out well in the Rutland area and then it spread to other parts of Vermont. The State Department of Education liked the idea and we had final contests take place in the State Capital, Montpelier. On April 12, 1984 the White River Valley Herald printed a picture of me as the Pronouncer of our State Finals in the legislative chambers of the Vermont State Assembly.

PHOTO BY ROBERT EDDY

Spelling at State Finals

Brian Townsend stands to spell a word for Allen Sher in the legislative chambers of the Vermont State Assembly in the state spelling finals Saturday. Randolph's seventh and eighth graders finished second.

To show that the Kiwanis Club supported the idea of Spelling Contests, we formed a team of our men and challenged the Rotary Club to a spelling competition. In the Fall of 1977, Rotary accepted and a large audience gathered in the Auditorium of the Rutland High School for this event. Rotary won but Kiwanis challenged the decision of the judges. Who won the Spelling Contest was referred to the Legal Committee, but we haven't had an answer yet.

Members of the Crossroads Arts Council saw how competitive adults can be when it comes to spelling. The Council planned to use it as a fund-raiser and it worked out very well. They formed teams of lawyers, doctors, teachers, bankers, realtors, storekeepers, etc., and the spellers studied a list of words that we prepared for them. A selling point was: spell it right, you score two points for your team; make a mistake, you receive no points but you are not out of the game. Each team paid an entry fee of $300.00 and we ran the Spelling Contest in the Fall of 1981 in Rutland with twenty three teams. A picture in The Rutland Daily Herald showed a check of $6,675.00 we raised from the Spelling Contest.

RUTLAND DAILY HERALD, MONDAY MORNING, DECEMBER 28, 1981

Spell $6,675

(Photo by Yvonne Daley)

Crossroads Arts Council raised $6,675 in its recent spelling bee fund raiser. Crossroads' organizers joined together for a luncheon Wednesday and the official presentation of the check. Pictured here, left to right, are Bob Condon, Allen Sher, Fran Veller, Sue Darrow, Sandy Cohen and Polly Wright with Nancy Beauchamp and Bob Goss in the foreground.

In 1976, I became Secretary of the Kiwanis Club of Rutland, was elected as Vice President in 1980, and became President for the term 1981-1982. Kiwanis has been an important part of my life because I believe in the focus of the members which is to help others.

Another way of helping others was to introduce folk dancing to people who had never danced. At the College of St. Joseph, I taught folk and square dancing to student teachers as an example of Social Recreation. I hoped that the teachers would use dance in their teaching because it was easy to correlate folk dancing with the Social Studies. In fact, the thesis I wrote for my Doctor of Education degree dealt with units of work and how teachers could reach their objectives by combining folk dancing with social studies and physical education. I recommended books in which instructions for the dances were given plus the names of companies that produced records with the music of the dances.

In 1982, nuns of the Sisters of St. Joseph in Rutland invited me to lead them in an evening of folk dancing. They asked me to come to their convent and we had fun doing the Hokey Pokey, Jessie Polka, Alley Cat, and Virginia Reel. Some of the nuns were teachers and planned to use these dances in their schools. The Rutland Daily Herald sent a reporter to cover this event and they printed a picture of me and the nuns doing the Alley Cat in their paper on January 5, 1982.

RUTLAND DAILY HERALD, TUESDAY MORNING, JANUARY 5, 1982

Dancing Nuns

Recently, the Sisters of St. Joseph met at the Mount St. Joseph Convent for an evening of folk dancing. Dr. Allen Sher, teacher at the College of St. Joseph the Provider, supplied the instructions and music for all of the dances. Everyone had fun doing the Hokey Pokey, Jessie Polka, Alley Cat and Virginia Reel. During the breaks, there was popular music for social dancing and there was good participation for the waltz, foxtrot and rock and roll. Some of the sisters plan to use folk dances in the classroom as part of the physical education program.

Since Rutland had the College of St. Joseph, and Castleton, only ten miles west, has Castleton State College, there were opportunities for adults in southern Vermont to take courses in Education. For full time teachers, there were Education courses in the Evening Division and also in the Summer Session. Delta Kappa Gamma was a sorority of women in Education and they asked me to be a guest speaker at one of their meetings. They wanted to know more about the Spelling Contests for adults. I gave them the information on competitions between adults and I added some anecdotes about intergenerational contests we had. In 1987, there was a contest between the POULTNEY Women's Club and the

CASTLETON Women's Club. I was the Pronouncer and it became a friendly and sociable competition. We also had intergenerational contests when we had seniors and children on the same teams. This was always a good-natured event because whenever a speller was correct, someone would lean over and give you a friendly pat-on-the-back. The youngsters would always smile and do their best to spell the words correctly.

Norwich University in Northfield, Vermont had workshops in 1986, called "Exercising the Good Life". Teachers from all over Vermont came to the university, and listened to experts who stressed that exercise can make your life better. After the speeches, the audience broke up into groups where they actually did the activities. I was the leader of "Folk Dances for Senior Citizens" and I showed these teachers how to do folk dances that were suitable for older people.

In the 1980's, Kiwanis International allowed women to join Kiwanis clubs. Some men objected but it was approved and this change has been a positive factor in the growth of the organization. In 1989, Ruth was sick with pneumonia and the doctor recommended that we move to a warmer climate. We chose North Carolina as our destination, and spent five years in Hendersonville, joining the Kiwanis Club of Hendersonville and getting involved in the community there.

Games Magazine in its September 1981 issue printed five quizzes that dealt with words. I had submitted the material to the magazine and they supplied the art work to attract the attention of their readers. *Games Magazine* paid me $125.00 for my efforts and it was one of the happy occasions when I received a check for my work. It made me think of all the experiences of my youth, when along with my brother, we did a variety of things to bring money in to help our family.

On November 22nd 1976, my 55th birthday, I was eligible to receive pension checks from the Teacher's Retirement System of New York City. It took time for the system to process my application. The first check did come in July 1977 and Ruth and I celebrated. We went to the Holiday Inn for lunch and we each had a Manhattan cocktail with our meal. When I think of 90 years of memories, I recall some days that were sad and some that were happy. This was one of our happy days.

CHAPTER 9

Exploring Vermont

In Rutland, we attended services at the Jewish Center. It was the only Jewish Congregation in the city and Ruth and I became members, even though it was a conservative congregation, led by a rabbi who leaned towards the orthodox point of view. We were able to help occasionally and assisted in leading activities for a dance of the Youth Group.

In 1976, I taught Israeli folk dances using my Califone record player and records I had brought from Laurelton. One event we planned was a Purim Party at the Rutland Jewish Center. We became good friends of Ruth and Sol ROSENBERG and at Passover, they would come to our house for a Passover Seder, and the following year, we would go to their house for the Seder.

Vermont is called the Green Mountain State and is known for the tree-covered peaks that run the entire length of the state. The beauty of the mountains helps make Vermont one of the most scenic states and yet it is low in the number of residents, being the 49th state in population. The only state that has fewer people than Vermont is Wyoming. It is a pleasure to drive to the different parts of Vermont and in the twenty years we lived there, Ruth and I managed to cover all corners of the state.

We've been to the northeast corner to visit Beecher Falls. In 1973, there was a gasoline shortage and thrifty Vermonters cut down on the oil and gasoline they used. The Ethan Allen Furniture Company in Beecher Falls was using oil to heat their factory.

They decided to use scrap lumber instead of oil. It worked well and they reduced the amount of oil they used. Some environmentalists, however, complained about burning wood and sending smoke and ashes into the sky. Most people did not object because our government was asking us to do this. Furthermore, the northeast section of Vermont had very few towns and not many people. It did, though, have many of nature's benefits: trees of all kinds, flowers, wild animals for hunting, streams for fishing and lakes for boating. We didn't think the people of the area would object to a little smoke from the furniture company. To verify this, we drove on US 5 along the Connecticut River to St. Johnsbury, the maple syrup capital of Vermont. On Railroad Avenue, we stopped at a diner for lunch. The menu featured pancakes and maple syrup. The price for three pancakes was $1.25 but the price of syrup varied according to the grade of syrup you chose. Grade C was 25 cents, Grade B was 50 cents, Grade A was 75 cents, and the best quality of maple syrup was $1.00. While we were there, we visited the Maple Syrup Museum and observed how important the sugar maple trees are to the farmers of Vermont.

From St. Johnsbury, we went on Route 114, a picturesque but unpopulated area of forty miles, due north to Norton. Norton is on the border of Canada and there is a customs office checking people who want to cross into Canada. As we approached this check point, Ruth noticed a very colorful church on a dirt road to our left. She asked me to drive down the road so she could take a picture of it and do a painting of it some day. Afterwards, we turned around to head east to Beecher Falls. As we passed the customs offices, we stopped so she could use the rest room. While I waited for her, a customs agent came over and asked, "Where have you been?" I told him we had gone down the dirt road to take a picture of the church. The officer said I had crossed into Canada without reporting to the officials. I asked him, "How did you know we had crossed into Canada?" He said there is an electric eye on that road and when I passed through the beam, an alarm sounded in the customs office. If we hadn't returned to Norton, he would have notified the Royal Canadian Mounted Police and when they stopped us, we would have been fined $500. Phew!

From Norton at the Canadian border, we drove due east on US 114 to Beecher Falls. We agreed that the Ethan Allen Company was acting wisely in burning left over wood in place of using heating oil. On our way back to Rutland, we passed through the town of Irasburg to see where the author, Howard Frank Mosher, lived. Ruth and I had read several of his books:

Where the Rivers Flow North
Marie Blythe
The True Account
A Stranger in the Kingdom
On Kingdom Mountain

We enjoyed them all. They were not only good stories but were very colorful and replete with the nature of northeast Vermont and the people who were permanent residents.

We traveled many times into the northwest corner of Vermont. Ruth and I went north on US 7 through Brandon to Middlebury, the home of Middlebury College. We went to Burlington, the state's largest city, home of the University of Vermont. Burlington is on Lake Champlain and there are large boats which carry people, trucks and buses across the lake to Plattsburgh, New York. North of Burlington is Essex Junction, home to a big IBM factory. St. Albans, VT, is a small city but is remembered for an incident of the Civil War in which soldiers from the south robbed the banks of $208,000 and went north, escaping to Canada.

I've been to Highgate Springs, VT, on Lake Champlain, close to Canada, to be the Pronouncer for a Spelling Contest. It was for people on a bus tour sponsored by McBride Group Tours. They were staying for three days at The Tyler Place and the organizer of the tour called me to lead the contest as a recreational activity. It was a very effective novelty and the guests had a good time with the concept of a spelling contest rather than a spelling bee.

Area Spelling Teams Assembling For Annual Crossroads Competition

Participation in the fifth annual Crossroads Arts Council Spelling Contest has grown to 30 teams, including all eight area high schools, as preparations for the first round on April 3 continue.

A steering committee consisting of Dr. Allen A. Sher, Fran Veller and Sandy Cohen is continuing to round up teams from area businesses and community groups and to solicit contributions for support of the contest.

Twenty-two adult teams and eight high school teams have so far agreed to participate. Each adult team will contribute $300. Private contributions will pay the entry fees for the high school teams, which will have their own separate division.

Adult teams will face off the evenings of April 3 and 10 at Rutland High School, with the top teams reaching the finals on April 17. The high school teams will have a preliminary round April 3 and finals April 17.

The format for the contest calls for teams of five members, four of whom participate at any one time. Eighty percent of the words come from a list given to all spellers in advance. The remainder are from a bonus list known only to the judges. Some brain teasers from previous years include "cicerone" (a guide for sightseers), "cartilaginous" (pertaining to cartilage), and "mithridatism" (tolerance of a poison acquired by taking gradually larger doses of it).

Students of Sher's word lists would recommend memorizing "phthisic" (pronounced tiz-ik, an archaic name for asthma).

Proceeds from the contest will support the Crossroads "Artists-in-the-Schools" program. The goal this year is to support 90 performances and seven "artists-in-residence" for 26,000 schoolchildren in the region.

Last year's contest netted more than $10,000.

Dr. Allen A. Sher displays a look somewhere between impish and devilish as he looks up from his big dictionary, one of the sources for "bonus" words in the coming Crossroads Arts Council Spelling Contest. Sher is in charge of preparing the lists of words.

This year's competition is dedicated to the late Robert S. Goss, who conceived the idea of using a spelling contest as a Crossroads fund-raiser. Goss, who died of cancer in December, was a former professional singer and actor and a strong supporter of the arts in the Rutland area.

Sher has been the prime mover of area spelling contests for a number of years, beginning with a spelling bee between the Kiwanis and Rotary clubs in 1977. His interest is beginning to pay dividends. He has been recruited as pronouncer for an island-wide contest for senior citizens in Bermuda and will travel there in May to preside.

Anyone interested in entering a team should call Fran Veller at 775-6000 before March 15.

Word lists will be distributed two weeks before the first night of spelling.

There were prizes for the top three spellers and after every inning, the scorekeepers announced the score. At one point, as we were waiting for the score, I told the audience that as I was driving north, I had the car radio on for a little music. At 10AM, the music ended and a program came on to help women with their cooking. The hostess said, 'Today, I'm going to teach you to make ratatouille". It is something like a vegetable stew made with eggplant, tomatoes, squash, onions and other vegetables. While waiting for the scorekeeper's total, I asked the audience, "Can anyone spell ratatouille?" One woman stood up and rattled it off perfectly, "R-A-T-A-T-O-U-I-L-L-E". People asked her, 'How did you know such a hard word?" She answered, "I often make it when eggplants are ripe."

Ruth and I also visited Montpelier, Vermont's capital. It is the smallest capital in the United States with a population of only 8,000 residents. Vermont is so small that you get to know the politicians and call them by their first names. I knew Governor Richard Snelling, whom we called "Dick", Governor Madeleine Kunin, whom we called, "Madeleine", Governor James Jeffords, whom we called "Jim", the Mayor of Burlington, Bernard Sanders, whom we called "Bernie", and the Mayor of Rutland, Gilbert Godnick, whom we called "Gillie".

In 1981, Ruth and I were on a state committee that was studying the health problems of senior citizens. We planned to drive to a meeting of the committee which was to start at 8:30AM in Montpelier, a one hour-twenty five minute drive from Rutland. We were ready to leave at 6:45AM because I wanted to stop for gasoline. It was in February and the temperature was 14 degrees below zero. The attendant was filling the gas tank and in talking about the weather, he said when he left his house in Fair Haven, it was 19 degrees below. The car felt good with a full tank of gas and we headed east on US 4. When we reached the town of Mendon, I felt the car wasn't giving us power. As we were going uphill, I pressed down on the gas pedal but the car sputtered and stalled. I pulled off the road, turned the key in the ignition and the car started. After two minutes of driving, the car stalled again and I said to Ruth, "We're not going to make it to that meeting in Montpelier." I turned the car around and drove downhill into Rutland, to the dealer where we had bought our Plymouth Valiant. He told us to drive it into an enclosed area where he repaired cars. He gave us a rental car and told us to come back the next day. On the following day, our car was working fine and his explanation was that there was water in the gasoline tank, the water had frozen into pellets of ice, and the ice was blocking the fuel line. He recommended that we add a can of Dry Gas every time we filled the gas tank. That was good advice and we never had that trouble again.

Rutland to Bennington is a picturesque drive because you go south and pass through Wallingford, Danby, Emerald Lake State Park, Manchester and Arlington. From Bennington, we've gone east to Brattleboro, driving on the Molly Stark Trail past Marlboro, the home of the Marlboro Music Festival. One morning, we stopped at Marlboro to buy 2 tickets for the Saturday concert. They were all sold out for the weekend, the ticket seller told us. As we talked, I heard music coming from the auditorium. "What's that?", I asked. "Oh, that's just a rehearsal. You may go in if you wish", came the reply. Ruth and I sat down with a handful of other spectators and listened to the orchestra as they practiced. The group finished and for the next number, a conductor came on stage. He was ninety year-old Pablo Casals, the world famous cellist. He seemed unsteady as he came on stage, but when he sat on a stool and picked up his baton, he became a vigorous, spirited conductor. At times, he'd stop and ask the orchestra to speed up the tempo or to play a section softly or with a staccato effect. Ruth and I were overjoyed at being able to see and hear Maestro Casals conduct this orchestra in such an intimate setting.

As a Professor of Education at the College of St. Joseph, I would arrange to place our seniors as student teachers. Once they were assigned to their schools, I would visit them and observe how they were doing with their teaching. I came to learn the roads of the southern half of Vermont as I traveled to the different schools.

The elementary school in Chester, VT was always happy to receive one of our student teachers. When I drove to Chester, I'd take State Route 103 and I would pass through the city of Ludlow. On the main street, I would drive by the law offices of Dan KESMAN. Every time that I passed his building, I noticed a Chrysler auto with the license plate BRA 36 parked in front of his office. I thought the car belonged to his secretary and I thought the tag might have referred to her brassiere size! One day, I saw Danny in Rutland, and I asked him what the license plate BRA 36 meant. He said it was his car and that he had gone to the Black River Academy in Ludlow and, that he graduated in 1936.

Ray Hull calling dances at Tunbridge.

One of the happy days of our life in Vermont was in October 1984 when Ray HULL, President of the Ed Larkin Contra Dancers, invited Ruth and me to join the group. Most of the people were farmers from Central Vermont and they met once a month in Chelsea or East Bethel to review the contra dances they had learned and to rehearse new dances that they wanted to perform for public appearances.

We came from Rutland, one hour away, on the other side of the mountain, but we did not mind the time

RUTLAND, VERMONT, FRIDAY MORNING, SEPTEMBER 15, 1989   COPYRIGHT   VOL. 132 — NO. 221

Staff Photo by Albert J. Marro

Dancing at the World's Fair

Glenn Button of Tunbridge swings his partner during the first set of dances by the Ed Larkin Contra Dancers Thursday morning at the 118th Tunbridge World's Fair. The group has been performing at Tunbridge since 1934 and will dance four times daily during the fair. *(More photos, Page 8)* spent in travel. It was a novelty to do contra dances and it was fun to become friends with a new group of people. As Ruth and I improved in our dancing, we became confident in our ability and were chosen to perform frequently. The biggest attraction of the year was dancing at the Tunbridge World's Fair, shortly after Labor Day. We would save our finest antique clothing for Tunbridge and we always made a hit with the audience.

While dancing at the Tunbridge Fair was a super attraction, we performed in all parts of Vermont, entertaining the public. Ruth worked on a book that gave the history of the Larkin Dancers and she described the members of the group, the dances we performed, and the communities where we demonstrated our programs. From her book, *And Everyone Would Sashay*, which was printed in 1989, I can list fifty six cities, towns, and communities of Vermont where the Larkin Dance Group danced:

Allen and Ruth dressed for dancing at the Tunbridge Fair

Barre	Ferrisburg	Poultney
Barton	Greensboro	Quechee
Belvidere	Guildhall	Randolph
Bethel	Hartland	Royalton
Bradford	Highgate Center	Rutland
Brookfield	Johnson	Sharon
Brownsville	Killington	Shelburne
Burke	Lake Willoughby	South Hero
Burlington	Londonderry	South Manchester
Calais	Ludlow	Swanton
Chelsea	Lunenberg	Tunbridge(World's Fair)
Cornish	Middlebury	Waitsfield
Danville	Montpelier	Warren
Dover	Morrisville	Washington
East Burke	Newbury	Wells
Enosburg	North Calais	Weston
Essex Jct.	North Clarendon	White River Junction
Fairlee	Northfield	Wilder
	Pittsfield	Woodstock.

In addition to the places where we danced in Vermont, I visited other towns and cities in connection with spelling contests, teaching folk and square dances, lecturing, doing storytelling, and teaching Jewish and Israeli dances. Keeping a calendar all these years, I look back fondly on all of our travels and activities.

A special day for myself and Ruth was Saturday, January 25, 1986. This occasion was our fortieth wedding anniversary. Most people wait for their fiftieth anniversary to have a gala celebration, but being in good health and spirit, we decided not to postpone this event. There were eighteen people who came to our Saturday night dinner party at Ernie Royal's Restaurant:

Fritzie and Joe Cohen
Clara Eisen
Rabbi and Mrs. Solomon Goldberg
Dory, Paul and Emily Gruber
Janice Hohenstein
Sara, Frank and Emma Mainolfi
Ruth and Sol Rosenberg
Anita, Steve, Allison and Marc Sher

Though we had planned the dinner for Saturday night, we entertained the guests at our home on Friday and Sunday. I have pictures of Allison and Marc playing Tower Ball and of Marc and me playing Korean Yoot. Ruth and I were involved with the Ed Larkin Contra Dancers and Ruth showed her antique dresses and hats that she wore to our dances, and I showed my frock coat, vest and high hat. Marc was intrigued by my high hat and wanted to see how he looked wearing it. I have a picture of Marc wearing my high hat with me standing beside him wearing my black derby. Ruth played popular songs on our piano and people gathered round for an old time community sing along. Ernie Royal's dinner was superb and it concluded with Baked Alaska for dessert. Emily, age 4, couldn't get over this dessert and she kept saying, "The ice cream's on fire!"

Some examples of Vermont Humor

1. Emory Hebard had a general store up north in Glover, VT, an area that is good for hunting and fishing. A salesman came in one day and sold Emory three dozen fishing lures, that were very good for catching bass. They were attractive items and Emory sold them all. Two weeks later, some fishermen came into the store and said they hadn't caught any bass with these lures. The next time the salesman came in, Emory reported this information. The salesman answered, "Well, Em, you didn't catch any bass but you sure did catch some fishermen".

2. Three men were in the maternity ward in the hospital in Randolph, VT. A nurse went to Mr. Jones and said, "Congratulations, you're the father of twins." "Wow", he said, "Isn't that a coincidence? I'm a pitcher for the Minnesota Twins." Fifteen minutes later, the nurse congratulated Mr. Brown. "You are the father of triplets". "Wow", he said, "Isn't that a coincidence? I work for the 3M Company". The third man became agitated and started to leave. The nurse asked him, "What's the trouble?" He said, "I'm getting out of this hospital. I work for 7-Up!"

3. Two elderly ladies drove down the main street of Middlebury, VT, and the driver made an illegal turn. A policeman noticed this and blew his whistle. She ignored the whistle and continued to poke along. They finally stopped and the officer came charging up and yelled, "Didn't you hear my whistle?" The driver looked up at the cop, fluttered her eyelids, and replied, "Yes, I did officer, but I don't flirt while I'm driving".

4. The Abenaki Indians needed a new chief of their tribe. The elders met and eliminated all but two contenders, Falling Water and Falling Rock. They announced a contest. Each was to go out hunting and the one who brought home more meat in one week would be the winner. Falling Water returned in one week with hides of deer meat but Falling Rock did not return. They looked all over for him but they couldn't find him. They made Falling Water chief of the tribe. They never did find the other Indian. In fact, if you are driving some roads of Vermont, you still see signs that say, "Watch for Falling Rock".

5. A train was going from Bennington to Rutland and the conductor came through to collect the tickets. An elderly farmer searched through his pockets and couldn't find his ticket. A man from across the aisle laughed and said, "Say, old timer, you're holding it in your teeth." The conductor looked down, punched the farmer's ticket and went into the next car. The man said, "You'd betta watch it. That's mighty careless being absent-minded like that." The farmer said, "Absent-minded nothing. I was chewing off last year's date."

6. A farmer, in bib overalls, from Shrewsbury, went into Gloria's Corset Shop in Rutland. He stood in the aisle, looking helpless, until a saleswoman came up to him. "I want a corset for my wife." The woman asked, "What bust?" "Nothing bust", said the farmer. "It just wore out."

7. Cleg Marshall in Chester, VT, had an ancient kitchen clock, so old that it kept bad time. He and his wife were in the living room, reading the morning paper when the clock struck twenty five times. Cleg put down the paper, took off his shoes, and said to his wife, "Sarah, we'd better get to bed. I've never known it to be so late."

8. Martha Green was an attractive lady from Hancock, VT. She worked as a social worker and often had to drive on dirt roads.

One hot, dusty, summer afternoon, she was passing a pond when she decided to go in for a dip. She piled her clothes on the bank and then waded into the water. She stood there knee-deep, enjoying the water when she heard a twig snap in the bushes behind her. "Who's there?" she called out. "Henry", a voice answered. Martha couldn't tell if it was a boy or a man. "How old are you Henry?" The voice answered, "85, dammit!"

9. Frank Spooner from Rochester, VT goes to the doctor for a general check-up. Everything is ok but the doctor says, "Frank, you're overweight. I recommend that you go jogging two miles a day for one hundred days. In 3 months, let me know what's what." Three months later, Frank calls the doctor and says he's been jogging two miles a day for one hundred days. The doctor says, "What's the trouble?" Frank answers, "I'm two hundred miles from Rochester. How do I get back home?"

10. At an auction sale in Tinmouth, VT, they put up an old decrepit horse for sale. A farmer watched as a young man in riding breeches and jodhpurs bid for the animal. The man bought the horse for a high bid of $85. The farmer said to the new owner, "What are you going to do with that horse?" The cocky fellow said, 'I'm going to race him!" The farmer looked at the horse, looked at the man and said, "You'll win."

11. Dr. Moseley had an office in Chelsea, VT and he was having a very busy winter. He had a horse and buggy and he'd go out on calls with his assistant, Jim Bronker. Late in the afternoon, they were returning to Chelsea and the doctor realized they were passing the house of Mrs. Holland. He told Jim to stop and he'd check on Mrs. Holland who had been sick for two weeks. Mrs. Holland was a large, well upholstered woman and she was lying in bed. Dr. Moseley felt her pulse and watched her breathing. He didn't believe in stethoscopes and he bent over and pressed his ear to Mrs. Holland's heart. He said, "Count slowly and don't stop until I tell you." Dr. Moseley was tired but he was so comfortable with his head on her chest that he fell asleep. When he woke up, she said, "5643,5644." The Holland family could never say enough about the times the doctor sat up half the night to make sure the patient was safe.

12. In St. Albans, VT, a judge in a domestic relations court was listening to both sides in the case of an older man who was charged by his wife with non-support. The judge considered the facts and said to the man, "You haven't taken proper care of the woman and I'm going to give her $100 a month." The man said, "That's mighty nice of you, judge. I'll give her a few dollars myself from time to time."

13. Jeffrey, an 8 year old boy from Essex Junction, went into Macy's Department Store in Burlington and headed for the lingerie department. He said to the sales lady, "I want to buy a present for my Mom. I want to buy a slip." The sales lady asked, "Is she tall or short? Fat or skinny?" the boy answered, "She's just perfect." The clerk picked out a slip, size 34, and put it in a box for him. Two days later, the Mother came into the store by herself and exchanged it for a size 52.

14. Hiram Clark has a farm near Orwell and called his doctor one night and asked him to come as soon as possible. The doctor said, "What's the trouble?" and Hiram responded, "My wife has appendicitis." "Nonsense", the doctor said, "I took out your wife's appendix three years ago. I never heard of anyone having a second appendix." Hiram answered, "Did you ever hear of anyone having a second wife?"

15. An elderly man was in the hospital in Waterbury, VT. One afternoon, the weather was good and he was walking near the building with a hospital aide. A bird flying overhead let loose and a dropping landed on the man's head. The aide said, "I'll go for some toilet paper." The man replied, "Don't bother. By the time you come back that bird will be half a mile away."

Some Calvin Coolidge Jokes

16. Calvin Coolidge was an example of dry humor. He was a man of few words. One Sunday morning he went to church alone. When he returned, his wife, Grace, said, "Did the minister preach a sermon today Calvin?" Calvin answered, "Yup." "Well, what was the sermon about?" "Sin." "Well, what did the preacher say about sin?" "He was agin' it."

17. Calvin Coolidge had a reputation as "Silent Cal". A woman at a party said to him, "I bet my husband that I could have a conversation with you for three minutes." Coolidge answered, "You lose."

18. Driving from Vermont to a meeting in Quebec in 1926, Calvin Coolidge passed into Canada. It was growing dark and they stopped at an inn in Sherbrooke. The clerk behind the counter asked Coolidge, "What is your name?" Calvin said, "It's printed on my valise." The clerk looked at the valise and wrote in the register, "Genuine Leather".

19. One Time That Calvin Coolidge laughed. Calvin Coolidge had a reputation for never smiling. In 1927, there was a reception at the White House and Will Rogers was invited to it. A reporter bet Will Rogers that he couldn't make Calvin Coolidge laugh. When Will Rogers was introduced to the President, poker faced Coolidge shook hands with Will. Rogers leaned over to the President, as if he hadn't heard and said, "Pardon me. I didn't get the name." Coolidge laughed.

20. President Coolidge once invited some friends to dinner at the White House. The friends were worried about their table manners so they watched Calvin and did everything that he did. All went smoothly until coffee was served. Calvin poured his into a saucer. The guests did likewise. Then he added sugar and cream. The guests did likewise. Then Calvin leaned over and gave it to his cat.

CHAPTER 11

Ruth and I Head South

In the fall of 1989, Ruth developed pneumonia and her doctor recommended that we move to a warmer climate. We thought of Florida, of Arizona/New Mexico, and of other parts of the south and we decided to explore North Carolina. After living in Vermont for twenty years, we had become accustomed to small cities, lots of green meadows, fields, trees, and cows, horses, and sheep. We also enjoyed the educational atmosphere of being near colleges, libraries, and the cultural presence of art and music. Driving south into North Carolina, we visited Chapel Hill – too busy, too many people, too many cars. We explored Durham and Duke University – too big, too commercial. We drove to Western North Carolina and browsed in Asheville. Again, too many vehicles. We drove south to Hendersonville and found a city of 6,000 people that we liked. Adjacent to Hendersonville was Flat Rock with Connemara, the home and estate of Carl Sandburg, and the Flat Rock Playhouse. We liked it! We stopped for gasoline in Hendersonville and when I filled the tank, I went to the office to pay. I gave the owner my credit card, he ran it through his machine and handed me the receipt, saying, " Y'all come back, you hear."That was such a hospitable way of saying, "Thank you" to a customer that I never forgot this southern cordiality. We certainly did come back.

Everybody in the U.S. came to know Sam ERVIN (1896-1985) when he was the Chairman of the WATERGATE HEARINGS in

Washington, DC. Sen. Ervin quoted from PROVERBS 17:22, "A merry heart doeth good like a medicine".

In 1973, my wife and I did not know that someday we would be living in North Carolina, Sam Ervin's home state. We listened to him and watched him on television and were impressed by his forceful and effective presentations before the U.S. Senate. In 1973, Sam Ervin was a U.S. Senator objecting to the fact that Pres. Nixon impounded highway funds that were to be used by the states. Sam Ervin joined the law suit to help N.C. obtain the money that had been allotted to it. There was a hearing on the impoundment of funds. Ervin said the president is entitled to give advice to Congress about the budget, but Congress doesn't have to take the advice.

"This reminds me of a story," said Sam in his N.C. accent. "An old lady came to see me in my law office in Morganton, NC, on a point of law. I took down some law books to verify my advice to her. I told her what her legal rights were. She started to leave and I said, "Just a minute. You owe me five dollars!" She said, "What for?" I said, "For my advice". She said, "Well, I ain't a-goin to take it".

Sam Ervin was a conservative Democrat, and when he spoke in the Congress he had a bit of folklore, or a story, or a line of poetry, for almost every subject. He was born in Morganton, N.C., had gone to the University of NC-Chapel Hill, and was graduated in 1917 with a B.A. degree. He volunteered for service in WWI in 1917, at age 21 and fought in the Second Battle of the MARNE. He was severely wounded in action and received the DISTINGUISHED SERVICE MEDAL. After serving in WWI, he went to Harvard University and received his law degree in 1922. He practiced law in Morganton for 30 years, served in the NC State Assembly, and was a judge in the N.C. Supreme Court. He served as a senator in the U.S. Senate from 1954 to 1974.

We moved to Flat Rock in 1990, sold our Vermont house, and bought a condominium in Hendersonville. There was no Reform Jewish Congregation in Hendersonville so Ruth and I drove to Asheville every Friday night to attend services at Congregation Beth Ha Tephila. One Friday evening at service, the president announced that we were going to have an interfaith activity with a catholic church in North Asheville. The members of St. Eugene R.C. Church had agreed to have a Passover Seder for their own people as well as ours on a Sunday afternoon, March 22, 1991. St. Eugene used the gymnasium of their school for these ecumenical events. They set up as many tables and chairs as they could, making accommodations for three hundred people. The women of both groups prepared the foods for the Passover Seder. We did not have a full dinner but we had a Seder plate on each table. As we read in the Hagadah about the foods and what they represented, servers in the kitchen brought out the food to the forty tables. At each table, there were women and men from each congregation and it turned out to be a friendly, educational, and very worthwhile activity for everyone.

In 1990, on the campus of Western Piedmont Community College in Morganton, NC, the Senator Sam J. Ervin, Jr. Library was dedicated. It is part of the college's library and is a replica of his home library. I have been to that library and I admired the senator's personal collection of books, professional and family memorabilia, and awards that Sen. Ervin collected over the years. On his desk, is a gavel that he used during the Watergate Hearings. It was given to him by the Cherokee Indians and it is decorated with Indian beadwork. Sen. Sam became recognized as an authority on constitutional law, and he gained national prominence as a defender of the Constitution. Some of the stories I use in my role as a guest speaker come from Sam Ervin's book, *Humor of a Country Lawyer* (1983).

I became active in the Kiwanis Club of Hendersonville and as I made friends there, I shared with them the Spelling Contests that had been so successful in Vermont. With the approval of the Board of Education, the Kiwanis Club sponsored Spelling Contests for children in grades 5 and 6, and for teenagers in grades 7 and 8.

One day, there was an ad in the paper by College Walk of Brevard, NC. They were having an Open House on Sunday and since Ruth and I did not have any appointments, we drove to Brevard to see their apartments and cottages. Sam HOWARD, a retired judge, and his wife, Helen, a retired teacher, were our chaperones and gave us an excellent tour. College Walk has an assisted living area and a nurse on duty day and night. The dining room and recreational activities were all so attractive that we put our names on the waiting list for a two-bedroom apartment. It happened that in two months, such an apartment became available and we moved into College Walk in June of 1994. There was room for Ruth to set up her paints and continue with her oil paintings and I had a room/office for my desk, books, and educational materials. There was a kitchenette for breakfast and lunch and Ruth loved the idea of not having to make supper. We had brought our electric organ from Rutland and Ruth entertained herself (and me) by playing and singing selections she knew from Gilbert and Sullivan, operas, and musical comedies.

The Transylvania Times, Brevard, N.C., Monday, March 30 ,1998-Page 7A

Spelling Across Generations
A fourth-grade member of the Spellcheckers team tackles a word during an intergenerational spelling bee held Friday afternoon at Pisgah Forest Elementary School. Fourth-graders at the school played with members of the College Walk retirement community in Brevard on two teams, with th second team dubbed as the Spellbeaters. The spelling be was sponsored by The Transylvania Times. (Times photo b Tracy Rose)

I was able to organize spelling contests between residents of College Walk and the faculty of Brevard College. We also arranged contests at elementary schools of Brevard and Pisgah Forest. We even had intergenerational contests where we had 3 senior citizens and 3 children on one team versus 3 seniors and 3 children on the other. Stella TRAPP, Publisher of *The Transylvania Times*, liked this way of helping children to improve in Spelling and printed articles and pictures of the events.

As I mentioned before, we drove to Asheville on Fridays to attend services at our congregation. When a couple had a special wedding anniversary, we always had a celebration. August of 1996 was a significant month for members of our congregation because there were eight couples that were married in 1946 and were celebrating their fiftieth anniversaries in 1996. World War II had ended in 1945 and veterans who were discharged in 1946 rushed to get married. The eight couples agreed to have a deluxe celebration in the Social Hall of the Congregation of Beth Tephila on Sunday afternoon, August 16. John COUTLAKIS of the *Asheville Citizen Times* came to our building and took a picture of each couple. The newspaper printed the eight pictures together with a colorful article by Carol CURRIE and this provided a memorable souvenir of that occasion.

Ruth was ill at that time but she said nothing was going to keep her from this anniversary party. We were both there to share in the festivities led by Rabbi Robert RATNER. Afterwards, Ruth continued to feel worse and after seeing several doctors, the diagnosis was cancer. She didn't smoke, she didn't drink alcohol, but somehow cancer hit her in the liver. She could barely eat and was admitted to Transylvania Hospital. She passed away on December 7, 1996 at the Ivy Hill Nursing Home.

Rabbi Ratner was very helpful to me in making plans for Ruth's funeral. The Morris Funeral Home on Merrimon Avenue in Asheville took care of the details and on December 10, we had a service there. I wondered if any people would come to this service, but many friends and relatives from Brevard, Hendersonville and Asheville did come to the service and to the burial at River-side Cemetery. The Sisterhood of our congregation prepared the meal of consolation in our Temple's Social Hall and I shall be eternally grateful to the women for arranging this ritual for me.

In January of 1997, I learned of a Support Group that met at the Presbyterian Church in Brevard. I joined the group of women and men who had lost their spouses and I did receive consolation from the people and from Reverend Marcus DODSON, who was in charge. I asked Rev. Dodson, 'When do you begin to feel better?" He very wisely answered, "I can't tell you when but you'll know when you feel better."

With Ruth gone, I began to experience what life is like when your spouse is gone. I tried to keep busy at the College for Seniors in Asheville, taking courses or teaching one. In addition to going to services every Friday evening, I participated in activities at our congregation that were helpful because they put me in contact with other men and women. I joined the Friendship Circle which met at the Temple once a month on Saturday mornings, I attended meetings of the Brotherhood and helped with their activities, and I shared in the work of the Social Action Committee. Once a month, women of the Sisterhood prepared a lunch for World War II veterans and I helped serve it to these men in need. Any time that we had outdoor activities like a hike or picnic, I would supply table games which people would play after lunch. At the Harvest House Senior Center, I enjoyed billiards, scrabble, pinochle, cribbage, and mixing with others in a class of folk dancing.

Senator Sam Ervin was a longtime member of the Kiwanis Club of Morganton, N.C. The KIWANIANS of Asheville have a deep regard for Sam Ervin, and for his interest in children. Our Kiwanis Club carries out some projects in schools and one of them is to sponsor PAWNDEMONIUM. This is a chess tournament for children in elementary, junior high, and senior high schools. We encourage them to have chess clubs in their schools and to play on a regular basis. The PAWNDEMONIUM is an event we sponsor once a year at the MONTFORD COMMUNITY CENTER. Over

100 students come here from all over Western NC and we supervise the tournament, consoling the losers and complimenting the winners. At the end of the day, we give trophies to winners in this chess tournament.

Another project related to school children is giving backpacks to needy girls and boys. One day in August, many KIWANIANS get together in the gymnasium of the Salvation Army. We form piles of school supplies: notebooks, pencils, pens, rulers, paper, etc. and we move down the line, putting one of each item in a brand-new backpack. Col. Ernie Miller of the Salvation Army and Scott Rogers of ABCCM supply the names of youngsters who need a backpack and we, of Kiwanis, feel good about carrying out the Kiwanis motto, WE SERVE.

The Spelling Contests for children is another activity that our club sponsors to help children with their school work. The principals and teachers of the CLAXTON School and the EMMA School have been very supportive. I have been the coordinator of these projects and have served as the Pronouncer in many Hendersonville and Asheville schools. The prize is a PIZZA PARTY to the class of the winning team. You can imagine how happy the class is that wins.

As I think of the people who have passed away because of cancer, I recall my daughter in California, Dory EHRLICH-GRUBER, who had cancer of the stomach. I flew to San Francisco to see her on May 1, 2008 and I was able to visit her in the hospital. As I left, she said, "I don't think I'll last another month." She was right and passed away in 15 days on May 15, 2008, leaving her husband, Paul and her daughter, Emily.

As one way of remembering her mother, Emily participated in the AVON WALK FOR CANCER. In San Francisco, this was a 39 mile walk that everyone did in two days, the Saturday and Sunday of July 15 and 16, 2009. To be eligible to be in the walk, the people had to solicit donations that would all go to cancer research. Each walker had to obtain a minimum of $1,800. in donations and this was feasible when people realized the money was to be used

105

for such a valuable cause. On Saturday, Emily and the others walked across the Golden Gate bridge to Sausalito, back to San Francisco, and then on the hilly streets of San Francisco for 25 miles. They camped overnight at a military base and then walked 14 more miles on Sunday. I was very proud of my granddaughter for completing this walk in memory of her mother, Dory.

An earlier trip that I made to San Francisco was in August 1997. My sister, Florence, and her husband, Ari, flew from Miami Beach to San Francisco to visit Ari's sister and her family who had a summer residence in Lake Tahoe, CA. Florence did not feel comfortable with California driving, especially since the road to Tahoe becomes mountainous east of Sacramento. "You know how to drive in the mountains because you did that so often in Vermont", she pleaded. It's very hard to resist my sister and I agreed to drive the 250 miles to Nevada.

Lake Tahoe is unusual in that some of the lake is in California and some is in Nevada. The city itself is on the very border and the part that is in Nevada permits gambling. We

Allen and his sister Florence

went to one hotel where there was a vertical line on the wall of the lobby. Arrows indicated where each state was. We had dinner in the California half and afterwards, Ari and Flo went into the Nevada half to play blackjack, roulette, and the slot machines. I am not a gambler and I sat in the lounge reading a book and hearing occasional yells when someone became a winner. On the next day, we went for a steamboat ride on the lake, and I was comfortable, knowing that somebody else was steering the boat. The water was so clear that we could see the bottom of the lake from the top deck of the boat.

When I returned to Asheville after that trip, I found a message from Marvin COLE who lives in Candler. We are both members of the Asheville Story-Telling Circle and Marvin is excellent in telling stories about Mark Twain. Marvin was President of the Candler Lions Club and he asked me to be the guest speaker at one of their monthly meetings. I agreed to do that for the club in November, and after dinner, Marvin introduced me for the evening's entertainment. I know many examples of Tar Heel humor and North Carolina folklore, some of which I'll share at the end of this chapter. I spoke for 20 minutes, and when the meeting ended, one member came over to speak to me. "Did you hear about the Baptist preacher from Lake Hominy?" Not waiting for an answer, he continued, "One Sunday, the preacher was going to talk about the evils of liquor. He went on for a good half hour and then in a loud voice, he said, 'If I had all the beer in the world, I'd throw it in the river!' After a pause, he roared, 'If I had all the wine in the world, I'd throw it in the river!' After another pause, the preacher thundered, 'If I had all the whiskey in the world....I'd throw it in the river!' The preacher then turned to the organist and said, 'What will our next song be for the congregation?' The organist replied, 'We Shall Gather by the River'."

When we moved to Western North Carolina, I continued some of the activities I had started in Vermont. I was able to do folk, square and contra dancing and the spelling contests for children and senior citizens. The Blue Ridge Center for Lifelong Learning in Flat Rock and the College for Seniors on the campus of the University of North Carolina – Asheville organized courses, lectures and trips that were of special interest to senior citizens. They looked for teachers and as I reviewed my qualifications and interests, I volunteered to teach certain subjects that I enjoyed and these were:

Railroads, Now and Then
Harry Golden and the Lower East Side
Poetry for Fun

107

Fun With Words
Driver Safety Programs of the AARP.

Playing pinochle and cribbage today are activities that I find very helpful. It is indeed fun to play cards and I enjoy these games in a variety of ways. They are sociable when we get together as adults and while playing, we swap jokes, we talk, talk, talk…about our families, our health conditions, our plans for going on a trip, local and national politics, the price of gasoline, etc. I find it gives me a chance to talk to others and for me to listen to them. At the Harvest House, a senior citizen's center in Asheville, I found a few people who like to play pinochle. This small group has been organized by Ann Marie BEHLING. We have increased to a dozen and we meet every other week in people's homes, have a pot luck lunch, and play pinochle. Ann Marie tells us the theme of the lunch and we all bring something appropriate, e.g., something red for Valentine's Day, something green for St. Patrick's Day, and red, white or blue for Flag Day.

Another group with which I play meets once a month on Wednesdays. It is organized by Gerry and Bill KOPACK and Eleanor and Frank LEMAY. We meet at noon at the house of the host or hostess, bring our own lunches, while the hostess provides a dessert and beverage, and then we have fun with pinochle. I learned pinochle as a teenager, playing with my father. As an adult, I learned how to play three-handed pinochle and in World War II, I played four-handed. Pauline CLARK taught me a different type of two-handed pinochle and we've had a lot of fun with her version.

In World War II, I learned how to play cribbage and I've found this to be an excellent pastime. When we lived in Vermont, we organized senior games that invited women and men to participate in a variety of physical activities. We called them the "Green Mountain Senior Games" and we had hundreds of people from all over the state register. One year, as an experiment, we offered cribbage as an activity, feeling that some older people may not want to take part physically but still would like the aspect of competition. There were

24 who signed up for cribbage and the winners happily received their gold, silver and bronze medals.

Here in Asheville, we don't have cribbage in our senior games but we do have a club that meets every Monday at 6 PM for spirited competition. Suzanne WYCKOFF organizes our games. We play weekly and have an annual picnic.

As I write of playing cards today, I recall card games we enjoyed as children, as adults, and as members of a family. The first game I learned was casino and I played that with my brother, Jack, and with friends on Cleveland Street in Brooklyn. Other games for two people that we knew were Concentration, War, and Rummy. Rummy had several versions and we also played Knock Rummy, and 500 Rummy. With a few people in a circle, we had games of Old Maid, Pig, and Fantan. We also gambled with cards when we played Poker and Blackjack. There were several types of Solitaire that were popular and we always chose easier forms so that the players would win more often than lose. I taught my son and daughter a solitaire game called Pirate Gold. They liked it because it was easy to win. From our cribbage group, I've learned a cribbage solitaire and a poker solitaire, both of which are fun to play, when I have time for solitaire.

In addition to playing cards, we liked table games. Some were for two people but others were for three or four. We amused ourselves with Chutes and Ladders, Sorry, Korean Yoot, and Five in A Row. We also competed at dominoes and here, too, we engaged in games for two or more.

A domino game that we enjoyed as a family was Honest John. When Ruth and I lived in Flat Rock, in 1991, we had a small apartment but the building had a large Community Room where we could play games or entertain guests. Anita and Steve, with their children, Allison and Marc, drove to North Carolina from Maryland for a visit and we relaxed in the Community Room. I suggested our favorite game of dominoes – Honest John – where all 6 of us could play. We had a great time that evening and the next day, Marc and Allison asked, "May we play Honest John again?"

109

As a teacher and recreation leader, I knew many games and in 1959, I submitted an article to The *Instructor* magazine with games that teachers could use. The *Instructor* printed my suggestions and these games were printed with instructions on how to play them:

Thanksgiving Relay
Seven Up
Detective
Supermarket
Snowman Relay
Baseball in the Classroom
Guess the Three-Syllable Word
Ringer Pass
Hide the Chalk
Catch and Drop Relay
Exercise to Rhythm
Things and Parts
Slide the Ring
EZ To Figure Out
Rhyming Words On the Board
Dog and Bone
Changing Seats
Angels Do It
Stand and Clap Relay
On My Way
Blarney Stone
Overhead Ruler Pass
Do You Have It?

In Asheville, the Parks and Recreation Department organizes Senior Games every year in May for women and men who are aged 55 years and older. There are track and field events, swimming races, cycling events, and other activities. I participated in the Green Mountain Senior Games in Vermont, in the Land of Waterfalls Senior Games in Brevard, NC and I registered here in Asheville, at the age of 90, for croquet, shuffleboard, horseshoes, and billiards. I was a winner and received a gold medal for winning in the 2012 Senior Games.

When we lived in Brevard, I did volunteer work

Allen at senior games

tutoring children in the Pisgah Forest Elementary School and in the Etowah Elementary School. In both schools, the children said the Pledge of Allegiance and then sang the N.C. State Song as part of the opening exercises. Bert RAMSEY, a native of North Carolina, went to school in Lenoir and tells that all children sang, "The Old North State" in the second and third grades. Bert sings our state song today with fervor and enthusiasm and complains that many adults who live in N.C. do not know their state song. Here are the words.

THE OLD NORTH STATE
By William Gaston (1778-1844)

Carolina! Carolina! Heaven's blessings attend her,
While we live we will cherish, protect and defend her,
Tho' the scorner may sneer at and witlings defame her,
Still our hearts swell with gladness when ever we name her.

Chorus:
Hurrah! Hurrah! The Old North State forever,
Hurrah! Hurrah! The good Old North State

One reason that many people of North Carolina today do not know their state song is that the song, "North Carolina Is My Home" has become so popular. This song has words written by Charles KURALT and music composed by Loonis McGLOHON.

111

At the request of Governor Jim Hunt, the two pooled their talents to honor the 400th Birthday of North Carolina, and here are the words to the song that they wrote in 1985.

NORTH CAROLINA IS MY HOME
Words by Charles Kuralt
Music by Loonis McGlohon

North Carolina is my home.
Here where the Smokies rise,
Here where the wind blows ocean foam,
Here where the wild swan flies.

Blossoms adorn the dogwood tree
Down on the old home place.
Tar on my heels feels good to me
Here in my State of grace.

Carolina raised me straight as a mountain pine,
Rocked me in her cradle, Southern mother mine;
North Carolina is my home, home far beyond all praise,
Goodliest home under Heaven's dome,
Here I shall spend my days.

CHAPTER 12

Some Examples of North Carolina Humor

1.Two men were hunting bear near Alexander in Mitchell County. They followed a mountain trail and came to a fork in the trail. A sign said BEAR LEFT. The men looked at each other, shrugged their shoulders, turned around and went home.

2.James GUDGER, a trial lawyer in Asheville, had a large practice in the area. In the 1920's, during prohibition, only druggists could sell liquor and that had to be for medical purpose and on the prescription of a doctor. One day, Jim Gudger drafted a document that looked like a prescription and he wrote on it, ONE PINT OF SPIRITUOUS Liquor. He signed it J.M. GUDGER, M.D. and sent it with a messenger to the drug store on Patton Avenue. A friend of Gudger's warned him, "You'll be in trouble representing yourself as a physician." Gudger said, "J.M. Gudger, M.D. doesn't mean that Gudger is a medical doctor. It means that J.M. Gudger is MIGHTY DRY."

3.Miss Gertrude GOODHEART was a woman of good standing in her church near Canton, N.C. She was about 40 years old, attractive, but not married. On the Sunday after her birthday, the preacher announced that Gertrude Goodheart had just had a birthday. In her honor, he asked her to choose three of her favorite hymns for that Sunday service. Gertrude was pleased. She stood up, looked around, and with her index finger, pointed to the best looking men in the church. She said, "HIM, HIM, AND HIM!"

113

4.At a Sunday School close to the Baptist Church of Brevard, a girl looked very sad. The teacher was aware of this and asked Mary, "Why are you sad?" Mary answered, "My cat died." The teacher explained, "Well, Mary, your cat is up in heaven with God." Mary answered, "What does God want with a dead cat?"

5.A few years ago, the speed limit on I 95 in North Carolina was 55 MPH. One man was going from South Carolina into Virginia and he was pulled over by a state trooper for speeding. The driver objected but the officer said, "You were clocked at 75 MPH." The man complained, "Impossible. I had set the cruise control at 70."

6.At the Post Office in Arden, N.C. there was a cheerful clerk. He weighed a package for a woman and said, "That will be $1.25." She gave him the money and he gave her the stamps. He said, "I can't lick those stamps for you....Do you know why I can't lick those stamps for you?" He paused, and without waiting for her answer said, "I don't have a liquor license."

7.Brevard has many new people in the summer because of the Brevard Music Festival. Last year a female violinist went to the SunTrust Bank to cash a check. She gave the check to the teller. He looked at the check then looked at the violinist. He said, "Can you identify yourself?" She opened her pocketbook, took out a mirror, looked in the mirror and said, "Yes, it's me."

8.Charley WHITMIRE of Franklin, N.C. was getting on in years. He went to his Episcopal minister and said, "If I leave all my money to the church, will I go to heaven?" The minister, quick of mind, answered. "I'm not sure but it's worth a try."

9.Amos GOSNELL lived near Burnsville, N.C. He was leading a flock of hogs down the road. He met a neighbor, Zeb ELLISON. They stopped to chat. Zeb asked Amos where he was going with the hogs. Amos answered, "I'm going about one mile down the road where there's some good pasture land." Zeb looked around and said, "Why do you have to go that far? This meadow is a good place for the hogs to eat. Why do you waste time going down the road?" Amos said, "What's time to a hog?"

10. Caleb SWANSON was 8 years old and lived in Charlotte, N.C. During the summer vacation, he spent a week with his grandparents who had a farm near Hendersonville. After raking, hoeing, and weeding in the family garden, Grandpa and Caleb went in a pickup truck to a garden center where Grandpa bought 6 bushels of manure. On the way home, Caleb kept sniffing the air and said, "Grandpa, what are you going to do with that?" He pointed to the manure. Grandpa said, "Well, Caleb, I'm going to put it on our strawberries." Caleb answered, "Is it all right if I have cream on mine?"

11. Judge Sam ERVIN was presiding in the County Courthouse of Hertford in Perquimans County near Elizabeth City. A man came before the judge to have his name legally changed. Sam asked, "What is your present name?" "Joseph Stinks". "Well", said Sam, "I can understand why you want it changed. Now, what would you like your name changed to?" "Well, judge, I'd like my name changed to Charlie. I really don't like the name of Joe."

12. Mrs. DOUGLAS went to the butcher in Skyland and asked for a chicken. The butcher went into the freezer, came out with his last chicken, put it on the scale and said, "That will be $2.75." Mrs. Douglas looked at it and said, "It's a little small. Do you have another one?" He said, "Surely" and went into the refrigerator again, came back with the same chicken and put it on the scale. Leaning on the scale with a heavy thumb, he said, "That will be $4.15." She said, "Fine, I'll take them both."

13.A reckless driver from Georgia was brought before a judge in Alleghany County for speeding. The judge saw it was an out-of-state driver and he delivered a sermon to the man. When the judge finished, the man said in a sarcastic tone, "You sure are an eloquent judge. I'll bet you can recite the Gettysburg Address." "I can", said the judge, "and I hereby fine you four score and seven dollars."

14. Jennifer BRONSON lived in Swannanoa and answered an ad for someone to work at a fruit and vegetable stand. She was interviewed by the owner. He told her what to do and as a test, he said, "What would you say if a man came up to you, pointed a gun at you and said, 'Put all the money in that cash register in a bag'." Jennifer said, "I'd say paper or plastic?"

Memories of Trips with Ralph Gray of College Walk

Ralph Gray and I became close friends through our living in the Main Building of College Walk in Brevard, N.C. Ralph and his wife, Jean, were retired but Ralph kept the skills he had acquired as an editor for the *National Geographic Magazine*. He spoke well and wrote with great knowledge of places he had visited. Our first meeting was when I was organizing a Spelling Contest as one of College Walk's recreational activities. It was going to be a team event and we had obtained six members of the faculty of Brevard College for one team and found six residents from College Walk who were brave enough to oppose them. Ralph was an excellent speller and I had to compliment him for his ability with words. After the competition between these two teams, we had senior spelling contests where people of College Walk spelled against one another. Ralph and I had fun with words and whenever we met, he had a challenging word for me and I had one for him in return.

The Parks and Recreation Department of Transylvania County had a Spelling Contest at one of its Senior Games and in May 1991, a dozen people registered for this event. Ralph was one of the spellers and he received a gold medal for having the highest score. When the closing ceremonies were over and the medals and ribbons were presented to the winners, the director announced an additional event: a canoe trip on the French Broad River!

Ralph had been on many canoe expeditions and he asked me if I wanted to go with him. I had been in rowboats but never in a canoe. "It's no problem", encouraged Ralph. "You sit in the front and paddle and I'll sit at the rear and I'll paddle and steer." I hesitated but Ralph was forceful and said we could certainly handle a canoe. There were 14 people who wanted to go on this three-hour trip, paddling downstream on the French Broad River. We all met

Ralph Gray being interviewed by WLOS ABC Reporter John Le at the College Walk Senior Spelling Contest, Brevard, NC, November 11, 1999

in Rosman at one o'clock, at the headquarters of the company that rented canoes and kayaks. An instructor gave a brief talk on water safety and then he showed a 10-minute film that told us what lay ahead. One of their guides came along in his own canoe to keep an eye on us if we had any trouble on the river.

Our canoe didn't seem sturdy and I thought it would surely tip over when I stepped into it. Ralph held one end, the guide held the other, and I managed to climb aboard and plop down on the front seat. Ralph nimbly stepped into the canoe, took his seat at the rear and we started to move. Every so often, Ralph told me what to do, and, believe it or not, we moved right along with the current. I found I could paddle and with Ralph in charge, we kept up with the other canoes.

At one point, there was a huge elm tree on the right bank of the river. It was tall and for some reason, it leaned to the left. Some branches were so sturdy that they dipped into the river. As a result of these limbs actually going into the current, half of the river was blocked and any people in canoes had to steer left to go around the tree. As we approached this tree, Ralph heard a bird overhead. The sound was unusually cheerful and Ralph looked up to see if he could identify the bird. As he looked up, he didn't look ahead and all of a sudden, the front of the canoe bumped into the branches. The current of the river turned our boat sideways and it exerted so much pressure, that the canoe overturned and tossed Ralph and me into the river. There was no danger because the river was only four feet deep but Ralph and I were thoroughly soaked and covered with mud. The guide paddled over to us, turned our canoe upright, and helped us climb back into our boat. Ralph steered us around the branches and we joined the others moving towards Brevard. I continued to face forward and felt an afternoon breeze hitting us. "How are you doing?" I called back to Ralph. He answered with chattering teeth, "I'm c-c-c-cold". I turned around and saw that his face was turning blue. I told this to the guide and he said, "Let's take him to Transylvania Hospital". There was a sandy section nearby and we pulled up onto it to get out of the river. Our guide went to a farmhouse and called his office for a station wagon. Ralph continued to shiver until the guide returned with some blankets from the farmhouse. The station wagon found us and took us to the hospital. They put Ralph in the Emergency Room and a nurse had Ralph take off his wet clothing and put on a hospital gown. Ralph's temperature was down to 94 and they covered him with heated blankets. After two hours, his temperature returned to normal and the nurse was ready to discharge Ralph. She went to give him his clothing and realized that everything he had was wet and muddy. Ralph gave me the key to his apartment and asked if I would bring him some dry clothing. Fortunately, I had my own car there and I drove to College Walk for his clothing, back to the Hospital, and then back to College Walk with Ralph.

College Walk has an Assisted Living section and they kept Ralph in one of their rooms overnight. It was 9:30 PM by this time and when I saw that Ralph was being supervised, I went to my apartment and changed out of my wet and muddy clothes. Since we hadn't eaten anything, I cooked some franks and beans and just as I sat down to eat, there was a knock on the front door. I went to answer it and found one of our nurses who had come to see how I was feeling. That was my first and last ride in a canoe, but I did go with Ralph to see other places in western North Carolina.

Many people recognize the phrase MANTEO TO MURPHY. Manteo is at the eastern end of N.C., touching the Atlantic Ocean while Murphy is 525 miles to the west very close to Tennessee and Georgia. There is one highway, U.S. 64,which goes across North Carolina from one end to the other, and if you stay on it, you will go from Manteo to Murphy. Ralph and I had been to the Outer Banks and had seen Manteo but we had never been to Murphy. We decided to do that and one day, drove on U.S. 64 west, through Rosman, Lake Toxaway, Cashiers, Franklin, and Hayesville to Murphy, the county seat of Cherokee County. One outstanding feature of Murphy is that the county courthouse is in the center of town and its outside walls are of shiny blue marble. We visited a museum that had artifacts of the area and we had lunch before leaving for Bryson City. Lunch was at a not-so-busy Long John Silver's and while we were eating our fish dinner, a woman came in with two boys, aged three and four. They looked as if they came from a farm with mother and children all wearing bib overalls. The boys ran between the tables and mother threatened them with, "If you don't sit down and behave, I'm not going to take you to Walmart." On our way to Bryson City, we passed through the towns of Marble, Andrews, and Robbinsville. Bryson City is the county seat of Swain County and has a cemetery where Horace KEPHART (1862-1931) is buried. We knew the name of Kephart because he lived in this area but preferred staying by himself in the mountains. He came from St. Louis in 1904 and for three years, he lived on the site of an abandoned copper mine on Hazel Creek.

In 1911 Kephart moved into Bryson City and the Cooper House became his permanent residence. In 1913, he wrote *Our Southern Highlands*, a book that is filled with anecdotes and folklore about the way of life in the Appalachians. It is a storehouse of knowledge about how to get along in the mountains. In his book, Kephart calls the remote area in which he lives, "The Back of Beyond". He even includes a chapter on how to make moonshine. Kephart wrote about a sheriff who roamed the hills and forests looking for illicit stills. When the sheriff came to a stream, he'd pause so his horse could drink water. If the horse shook his head and refused to drink, it was because the water contained refuse from a still. The sheriff would follow the water upstream until he found the still. The cemetery in which Horace Kephart is buried has a large plot overlooking the town and the mountains beyond, enclosed by a special picket fence. There is no usual cemetery monument but there is a huge ten-ton boulder on which there is a small plaque of lettering in bronze. The boulder is one that came from the mountains and represents the unusual life that Kephart led. One of Kephart's contributions was his energy in forming the Great Smoky Mountains National Park out of land that was being destroyed by the lumber interests.

From Bryson City, we entered the Blue Ridge Parkway, and followed the Parkway to its highest elevation, 6,047 feet, near Balsam Gap. We took winding route 215 down to Rosman and then home to Brevard.

Another frequently heard phrase is "Trust to Luck". In Madison County, there are two neighboring communities where one is named Trust and the other is named Luck. Ralph and I wanted to see these places and we planned a trip from Brevard to the western part of Madison County. We drove to Asheville, north to Alexander and then to Marshall, directly on the right bank of the French Broad River. Marshall is the county seat of Madison County, and the county courthouse is on Main Street facing the river. Marshall is about one mile long, one mile wide and is limited in size by the mountains and the river.

It is about 20 miles to Hot Springs on the left bank of the French Broad River. Hot Springs was originally called Warm Springs and it was in 1778 during the Revolutionary War that the Springs were discovered. Two American soldiers on the right bank of the French Broad River spotted a group of horses across the river. The horses had been stolen by Indians and the two scouts waded across the river to seize the horses. As they waded, they noticed that the water was unusually warm. It turned out that the area was fed by underground hot springs. Word about the springs spread and invalids came to bathe in the warm water, hoping that they would be healed. The town grew and in 1886, the name was changed to Hot Springs. The Appalachian Trail goes along the Main Street of Hot Springs but Ralph and I drove on 209 about 8 miles to Max Patch Mountain. It is 4,629 feet high and has a grassy bald at the top. It is called the crown jewel of the Appalachian Trail because of the panoramic view from the summit. In three miles, you reach the community of Trust which has a general store, a café, and the church, St. Jude's Chapel of Hope. From Trust to Luck is only 1.4 miles and Luck consists of just one store and a bridge. It did not take long to explore Luck and we headed home.

Linville, North Carolina is in McDowell County, three miles east of the Blue Ridge Parkway. Ralph and I wanted to explore the Linville Caverns and we drove about 100 miles on the Parkway to Milepost 305.9. The Linville River cascades 90 feet into Linville Gorge, a national wilderness preserve, second only to the Grand Canyon. Linville Caverns are a series of massive limestone caves where you can see stalactites and stalagmites. These centuries-old limestone pieces have unusual shapes and colors and some resemble fantastic animals. We followed the path along an underground stream and into several lighted chambers of the caverns. When we left the Caverns, we returned home on N.C. 181 to Morganton. We stopped for lunch at an unusual restaurant, located precisely where three counties meet. We sat at a table where directly overhead in the ceiling, was a marker, showing exactly where Avery County, Caldwell County, and McDowell County come together. We had lunch, with Ralph in one county while I was in another.

The trips with Ralph weren't always long-distance experiences, but there are many places in North Carolina where I had personal or educational business:

AHO, in Southern Watauga County, near Boone, is a community that did not have a name. A group of men met to choose a name and they just couldn't agree. They decided that they would accept the next word spoken by any of them. After a long silence, one man rose, stretched, and said, "Aho".

The Apple Festival takes place in Hendersonville for four days, ending on Labor Day. It celebrates the role of Henderson County as the major apple-growing region of North Carolina. On Friday, Saturday, and Sunday, Main Street is closed to traffic and vendors set up booths where they sell apples, cider, apple desserts, and arts and crafts items. Two high school students are chosen for King Apple and the Apple Queen, and they ride in an open car in the Apple Day Parade on Labor Day.

ASHE County was formed in 1799 from WILKES County and is bordered by the states of Virginia and Tennessee. It is named for Samuel ASHE, a patriot of the Revolutionary War, a superior court judge, and Governor of North Carolina from 1795-1798. Many dairy and agricultural items come from Ashe County and it has the only cheese factory in North Carolina, making Cheddar, Colby, and Monterey Jack Cheeses.

ASHEVILLE was incorporated in 1797 and was also named after Governor Samuel Ashe, as he was a very popular governor of that time. Railroads came to Asheville in the 1880's, bringing people and commerce to the area. Asheville is called "Queen City of the Mountains" and has the Biltmore Estate, the Thomas Wolfe Memorial, St. Lawrence Basilica, the first Roman Catholic church consecrated in North Carolina, and the Smith-McDowell Museum, the oldest existing brick house in the city, and McCormick Field, the home of the Asheville Tourists Baseball Team.

BREVARD, the county seat of Transylvania County, is 30 miles southwest of Asheville and is known for its annual Summer Festival of Music. There are performances of the Brevard Orchestra, opera, and chamber music. Brevard is in the Land of Waterfalls and has attractive scenery and pleasant drives.

BURNSVILLE is the county seat of Yancey County and is named for Otway BURNS, a privateer of the War of 1812. He lived in Beaufort, North Carolina and built a house with an observatory on top. Lookouts told him whenever an English ship was in sight. Burns built a very fast ship called the Snapdragon and with it he captured and destroyed many English ships. King George of England offered a price of $50,000. for the head of Burns. Although Otway Burns was an easterner, as a member of the state legislature, he supported the interests of the people of Western North Carolina. He moved to Burnsville and when he died, people erected a statue of him and placed it on their village green. He is wearing a naval uniform, has a cocked hat, and is holding a telescope. The base of the statue has the words,

SAILOR SOLDIER STATESMAN

HE GUARDED WELL OUR SEAS

LET OUR MOUNTAINS HONOR HIM.

CANNON VILLAGE occupies the center of the town of KANNAPOLIS, 26 miles northeast of Charlotte. It was built by Charles CANNON in 1887 and became a leading manufacturer of textiles, specializing in towels, linens, and blankets. There is an outlet store for Cannon Bed and Bath products.

CHEERWINE is a soft drink with a taste somewhere between Dr. Pepper and Cherry Coke. It is called the Carolina Chianti and is bottled by the Carolina Beverage Company in Salisbury,

North Carolina, 30 miles southeast of Statesville. Cheerwine started in 1917 at the time of World War I. There was a shortage of sugar and they used a wild cherry flavor to make the soda.

The CONFEDERATE MONUMENT in Hendersonville is a tall shaft of grey marble on the lawn of the Henderson County Court House. On it is the inscription "To the Confederate Soldiers". It was erected in 1900 and stood in the intersection of Main Street and First Avenue. In horse and buggy days, there was no trouble but when automobiles used Main Street the monument was a traffic hazard. In 1925, it was moved to the court house lawn.

CRAGGY GARDENS is at milepost 364 of the Blue Ridge Parkway, 25 miles northeast of Asheville. This area has an interpretive center, picnic area, hiking trail, and a forest of rhododendrons that blanket the mountain in June. These are not formal gardens but slopes of the Blue Ridge Mountains that glow when the flowers are in bloom.

EXUM is the name given to Lillian Clement Stafford. Her father, George CLEMENT came from Exum, North Carolina, 10 miles north of Calabash in Brunswick County. After the Civil War, he moved to Western North Carolina, became a foreman for George Vanderbilt, and helped to build the Biltmore House. Lillian was the sixth of seven children and was born in Black Mountain. She studied law and in 1916, passed the bar exam. She was the first female lawyer to practice without any male partners. In 1920, she was elected to the General Assembly by a vote of 10,368 to 41. She introduced 17 bills and 16 became laws that affect us today:

> People should have privacy in voting;
>
> Cows should be inoculated for tuberculosis;
>
> Traffic signals should have yellow caution lights.

Exum died of pneumonia in 1925 at the age of 31 and is buried in Asheville's Riverside Cemetery.

FRANKLIN is in Macon County, at the junction of U.S. 64, U.S. 23/441 and N.C. 28, and is called the "Jewel of the Southeast" because it is the center of a thriving gem-mining industry.

The COWEE VALLEY, just north of Franklin, has rocks that contain rubies, sapphires, and other gemstones.

Frescoes are paintings done by an artist on wet plaster. Ben LONG of Statesville, N.C. in 1980 did the frescoes on the walls of St. Mary's Episcopal Church and also at the Holy Trinity Episcopal Church, both near Jefferson, N.C. in Ashe County. The Holy Trinity Church has a large fresco of the Last Supper.

GINSENG, sometimes called "Seng", is a herb that people pick and sell at grocery stores. A pound of dried ginseng is worth about $20.00 and it takes three pounds of green 'seng to make one pound of the dried herb. It grows where there is rich dirt in the Blue Ridge Mountains and people harvest the root of ginseng, not the top. Horace Kephart says that seng is marketed only in China and it has many medicinal benefits: improves the blood and is good for the lungs and stomach.

HANG GLIDING is a busy activity on Jockey's Ridge, a sand dune 138 feet high, just north of Nag's Head on the Outer Banks. Francis ROGALLO, a nearby resident, invented the Hang Glider while he was doing work for NASA. The gliders are made of mylar and aluminum. Each year in May, there is a three-day competitive hang gliding contest. In 2007 when we were touring the Outer Banks, I climbed to the top of Jockey's Ridge and was very close to people who were practicing their hang gliding skills.

JOT-UM-DOWN, is a community in Surry County, east of Elkin and west of U.S. 601. It has a fire station with Jot-Um-Down painted on the station and on their four fire engines. The town has been known for over fifty years and owes its name to Zeb THOMPSON who had a grocery store there. When his customers bought food on credit, they would ask Zeb to jot-um-down and he would do so in a book that he kept for that purpose.

KILL DEVIL HILLS is a town in Dare County, on the Outer Banks. The name comes from the rum the people drank. It was so strong that people said it was powerful enough to kill the devil. The WRIGHT BROTHERS of Dayton, Ohio built a glider and tested it with a motor. It worked and on December 17th, 1903, it flew for

12 seconds, covering 120 feet. In other flights, Wilbur and Orville covered 852 feet.

LAKE TOXAWAY is in Transylvania County, 15 miles west of Brevard on U.S. 64. It is an artificial lake, one mile wide, three miles long, and has a shoreline of 14 miles. An earthen dam, 60 feet high and 500 feet long, created the lake. In 1903, the Lake Toxaway Inn was built. It was five floors high, and had 500 rooms, each with a view of the lake and mountains. The dam had a generator that produced electricity for the inn which had elevators, telephones, an orchestra in the ballroom and many outdoor activities. The dam broke in 1916 with pressure of a hurricane from the Gulf of Mexico combined with a storm in Western North Carolina. A new dam was built and Lake Toxaway was refilled.

LAKE NORMAN is about 20 miles north of Charlotte. It was formed in 1963 when the Duke Power Company built a dam on the Catawba River to generate electricity. The lake is the largest body of fresh water in North Carolina, and is named after Norman COCKE, a former president of Duke Power. The lake has 520 miles of shoreline and this makes it great for recreational boating.

LOAFER'S GLORY is a community in southwest Mitchell County, about 15 miles northwest of Spruce Pine. It was so named because when men finished their farm chores, they would gather on the porch of the general store to play checkers, spin yarns, whittle and throw horseshoes.

MAGGIE VALLEY is named for the daughter of the town's first postmaster. It is about 30 miles west of Asheville on U.S. 19, at the foot of the Balsam Mountains. It is a strip three miles long and has a small local population. Many are involved in the tourist trade and offer these attractions and events:

Ghost Town in the Sky – a theme park

Maggie Valley Opry House – bluegrass music

Soco Garden Zoo – small collection of wild animals

Stompin' Ground – a hall for cloggers

Folkmoot USA – folk dance groups from all over the world

Moonlight Race – an 8-10 km. footrace in August, at night

MAYLAND is an area of Western North Carolina that refers to the three counties of Mitchell, Avery and Yancey. Mayland Community College is in Spruce Pine. Mitchell County was named for Dr. Elisha MITCHELL, who showed that Mount Mitchell was the highest peak east of the Mississippi. Avery County was named for Col. Waightstill AVERY, a Revolutionary War soldier who became an attorney general of North Carolina. Yancey County is named for Bartlett YANCEY, a member of the State Assembly and a member of Congress.

MT. AIRY is in Surry County, about 60 miles north of Statesville on I-77, and just three miles south of Virginia. Andy GRIFFITH was born there in 1926 and the city has a huge granite quarry. The granite company supplied the stone for the State Capitol in Raleigh and for the Wright Brothers Memorial in Kill Devil Hills.

OWENS FOLLY is what the people of New Bedford, MA said when they heard that Charles D. Owen was looking for a factory in the south where he could make blankets. His son, Charles Owen II, chose the Swannanoa Valley, 10 miles east of Asheville, for their factory. It had a work force of 2,200 people and in World War II, Beacon Blanket Company produced 7 million blankets for the U.S. Armed Forces. Swannanoa named their high school, Charles D. Owen High School after the Owens Family.

PEARSON FALLS is a wildlife preserve, named in memory of Captain Charles William PEARSON, a native of North Carolina and a civil engineer who helped survey the route of the railroad from Salisbury, NC to Spartanburg, SC to Tryon, NC to Hendersonville, NC and then to Asheville, NC. In his surveying, he found the waterfalls that now bear his name. Land was cheap and he bought large acreage between Tryon and Saluda, NC including the land of the waterfalls. When Capt. Pearson died, his son owned the land and in 1931, he sold the land to the Garden Club of Tryon. The club named the waterfalls in honor of Charles Pearson and pledged to preserve and protect the native mountain flora. They built trails so that visitors can see the plants and waterfalls.

PEPSI-COLA was created in 1898 by Caleb BRADHAM, a druggist who had a pharmacy in New Bern, North Carolina. He concocted a new soft drink that he sold at the fountain in his drug store. They called it Brad's Drink but he didn't like that name and he bought the name Pep Kola from a New Jersey company that was defunct. He changed it to Pepsi Cola.

POOR STREET is named after William Probart POOR who was one of three men who did a survey for the town of Brevard, North Carolina. They chose Main Street and Broad Street as the center of town. Probart Street, Gaston Street and Jordan Street were named for these people. William Probart Poor was a merchant and had a store in what is now known as The Red House, 412 Probart Street. The street was originally known as Poor Street, named for the Poor Family. As people moved onto this street, they changed the name to Probart Street.

ROCKY MOUNT is a city in the eastern part of North Carolina, about 60 miles northeast of Raleigh. It is in two counties, Edgecombe County and Nash County. Railroad tracks go down the middle of Main Street and form the boundary line between the two counties. The city is named for the rocky mounds and ledges in this area, near the falls of the Toe River. Rocky Mount produces tobacco and furniture.

ROSMAN, 9 miles southwest of Brevard, is in Transylvania County at the intersection of U.S. 64 and U.S. 178. It was a busy city from 1906 to the 1950's with a sawmill, a tannery, and an extract factory. The Hendersonville-Brevard Railroad reached Brevard in1894 and went to Rosman by 1903. Rosman comes from the names of two associates of Joseph Silversteen, Joseph ROSenthal and Morris Or MANsky.

SANDY MUSH is a town in northwest Buncombe County, about 5 miles west of Leicester and one mile west of S.R. 63. It was named by an early hunting party when sand from the creek water

129

got into the mush they were cooking for supper.

SMITHFIELD is a town and county seat of Johnson County, about 20 miles southeast of Raleigh. It is named for John Smith, owner of the land on which the town developed. It is the home of the Ham & Yam Festival and is where Ava Gardner lived. There is an Ava Gardner Museum, featuring memorabilia and movies from Ava's Hollywood career.

SPENCER is the home of the North Carolina Train Museum, about 2 miles north of Salisbury. The Southern Railway built a repair facility there and today it has a display of railroad rolling stock. It also has a 45-minute train tour of the area.

TOM COLLINS lived in Balsam, in Jackson County, about 10 miles south of Waynesville, near Milepost 440 of the Blue Ridge Parkway. He came from Scotland and was one of the first settlers in Western North Carolina. Tom had a spring on his property and he became known for his concoctions: a jigger of corn whiskey, sweetened spring water, and a dash of bitters made from his elderberries. This was the origin of the Tom Collins we drink today.

TUXEDO is a town about 7 miles south of Hendersonville, on Lake Summit, just south of Flat Rock. It was originally called Lakewood but to avoid confusion with another Lakewood in North Carolina, the people changed the name to Tuxedo.

WANCHESE is a community in south Dare County, with a population of about 1,000 people, on the south end of Roanoke Island, about 5 miles south of Manteo. Wanchese was called the lower end of Roanoke Island while Manteo was called the upper End. Wanchese is an important commercial center for fishing on the Outer Banks.

WAVES is a community on the Outer Banks of North Carolina, 2 miles north of Salvo, and 2 miles south of Rodanthe. Its altitude is five feet and has a population of 65, more in the summer. A post office was established there in 1939 and they named it Waves because it is easy to say and because it is on the Atlantic Ocean, it does have plenty of waves.

WHYNOT is a town in south Randolph County, 2 miles

south of Seagrove and 10 miles south of the North Carolina Zoo in Asheboro. In the late 1800's, a group of local citizens met to choose a name for their post office. They heard many suggestions beginning with, "Why not name it for so and so?" In desperation, one man said, "Why not name it WHYNOT?" They did.

ZEBULON VANCE Homestead is 12 miles north of Asheville and is a North Carolina State Historic Site. It features the mountain home of Vance who was a colonel in the Civil War, a governor of North Carolina, and a U.S. Senator. There is a two-story main building and also a springhouse, a smokehouse, a loom house, and a tool house.

ZOAR is a community in Union County, about 25 miles southeast of Charlotte. Zoar in Hebrew means 'little' and it is a tiny village at the crossroads of S.R. 1118 and S.R. 1005, west of U.S. 601. The Zoar United Methodist Church is in South Carolina, one mile south of the N.C./S.C. border. A few stores operated at the crossroads but only one remains today. People of Zoar, on both sides of the state line, are buried in the cemetery of the Zoar Church.

CHAPTER 14

Fun With Words

A good part of my life has been connected with words – using words in teaching children, speaking to parents, or to people at large. Another aspect of words is *avocational* – doing crossword puzzles, cryptograms, and appreciating authors like William SAFIRE, Richard LEDERER, and Eugene MALESKA. With a collection of books by these distinguished linguists, I've assembled enough material to teach classes called "Fun With Words" and I'm going to share some of these items that have made people laugh.

BERRAISMS – phrases by Yogi BERRA who used to be a catcher for the N.Y. Yankees:
> No wonder nobody comes here – it's too crowded.
> I want you to pair up in threes.
> When you get to the fork in the road, take it.

GOLDWYNISMS – by Sam Goldwyn, producer of movies in Hollywood:
> A verbal contract isn't worth the paper it's written on.
> This book is too much plot and not enough story.
> I never liked you and I always will.

PALINDROMES – a word or sentence which reads the same forward or backward:
> For example:
> level, radar, Otto
> Madam, I'm Adam

REDUPLICATIVE WORDS – compound words that have two elements that are slightly different:

ticktock	wishy-washy
seesaw	helter-skelter

DYNAMIC TRIOS:

3 Fates	3 little pigs
3 Musketeers	3 wise men

ALLITERATION:

baby boomer	sweet sixteen
hitch hiker	pen pal

BLEND WORDS – two words joined to make one:

smog	infanticipate
cranapple (juice)	saniflush

BURMA SHAVE SIGNS:

Don't stick your elbow	Don't pass cars
Out too far	On curve or hill
It may go home	If the cops
In another car	Don't get you
	Morticians will

HOMONYMS:

carrot, carat, caret	rode, road, rowed
towed, toad, toed	pair, pare, pear

ONOMATOPOEIA:

fizz of soda	tinkle
clang of a bell	buzz

KNOCK KNOCK JOKES:

Sarah who?	Sarah doctor in the house?
Ken who?	Ken I come in?
Butcher who?	Butcher arms around me, honey

PSEUDONYMS:

| William Sydney Porter | O'Henry |
| Samuel Langhorne Clemens | Mark Twain |

PUNS:

My wife's gone	What's black and white
to the West Indies.	and read all over?
Jamaica?	A newspaper
No. She went	
of her own accord.	

OXYMORON – a figure of speech in which two contradictory terms are joined to form a pair of words that are opposite:

small fortune	plastic silverware
white chocolate	tight slacks
negative growth	

TOM SWIFTIES:

"Have a ride in my new ambulance", said Tom hospitably.

"I hate pineapple", said Tom dolefully.

"Pass me the cards", said Tom ideally.

HINK PINK – a pair of rhyming words, only one syllable long:

red light = NO GO

intelligent fish = SMART CARP

autumn dance = FALL BALL

group that eats at noon = LUNCH BUNCH

ELEPHANT JOKES:

Where do elephants store their clothes?

In their trunks.

How do you stop an elephant from charging?

Take away its credit card.

SIGN OF THE TIMES:
    At a restaurant/gas station – EAT HERE AND GET GAS
    In a maternity ward – NO CHILDREN ALLOWED
    In a funeral parlor – ASK ABOUT OUR LAYAWAY PLAN

MISSPELLING: I enjoyed reading Charles Kuralt's book, *On The Road With Charles Kuralt*. These are some examples of humorous misspellings he documented over the years: Our country shows refreshing evidence of individualism, as seen on roadside signs:
    PARK HEAR – spelled wrong, but it does tell you where to park
    MACHANIC ON DUTY. FRONT END REPAIRED – he may not be good at spelling
    but he's good at fixing cars
    ANTIQES
    SOUVINERS, SOVVENIERS, SOVVENIRES
    ACERAGE FOR SALE – this man's a farmer, not a teacher
    RASBERIES
    SPEGHETTI AND PIZZA
    BEER AVAILALBE HERE – sampled the product while painting the sign
    BAR DRINKS .55 ANEYTIME
    BE CURTEOUS AND SMILE – in back room of an Oklahoma diner
    BAR AND RESTRUANT – huge lighted sign in Oregon
    HUNGARY? MARION'S SNACK SHACK 6 MILES
    NO TRESSPASSING, NO TRASPASSING, NO TRUSTPASSING – just keep out
    NO BOATS ALOUD – silent boats, OK

NO CONGRETATING ON THE DRIVEWAY.
VIOLATORS WILL BE PROSCUATED.
(Fearing PROSCUATION, we didn't
CONGRETATE. We paid for our gas and
headed down the road).

• • •

In addition to teaching a variety of courses at the College for Seniors in Asheville, I did volunteer work for the Literacy Council of Buncombe County. The Council helps people from foreign countries learn English. In 2001, I worked with a man from Mexico, Geronimo CABRERA. He was about 40, had a full-time job working in a factory in Asheville, and he came to me for tutoring. When he left me, he usually went to a house where he did part time work, gardening and pruning of trees. After three years, he felt he had enough and the Literacy Council asked me to work with Alejandro PEÑA. Alejandro was in his twenties, also from Mexico, and worked for a textile factory in Weaverville. We'd meet in a corner of the Oakley Library and spend about an hour and a half each week. He made good progress with his oral and written English. Alejandro came from a suburb of Mexico City and his mother ran a grocery store there. He was hoping to learn enough here that he could teach English in a school in Mexico. Alejandro returned to Mexico and I worked with a different student, an American, the next time. The Craggy Correctional Center near Weaverville has inmates who need help with their education. There are many who are not high school graduates, and there were two teachers from A-B Tech who were assigned to full time teaching at the prison. They tried to help the inmates pass the test for a Graduate Equivalency Diploma. The man I worked with on a one-to-one basis was 62 years old and had never graduated from high school.

The Correctional Center has a library and I'd work with my student for an hour and a half each week. He had good handwriting but his spelling and grammar and punctuation were poor. I obtained workbooks and textbooks and I gave him a homework assignment each week. There was considerable improvement in his Reading and Writing. After I worked with him for a year, he was transferred to the Correctional Center near Spruce Pine. He wrote me a letter saying he had passed two parts of the G.E.D. and was working on the other two.

While I was tutoring people and conducting spelling contests, I belonged to T.A.P., The Autumn Players of the Asheville Community Theater. This is a group of senior citizens who like being dramatic and do so by reading poetry to people in nursing homes, acting in reader's theater plays, and by performing in plays. For two years, I went to the recreation rooms of several nursing homes. We'd go in groups of three and read poems that were seasonal, e.g., in October, we'd read poems about the Fall, in December, we'd read about winter weather and holidays, and in July, we'd read about hot weather and poems that dealt with swimming. After reading a poem, we'd ask a few questions and try to have the listeners share their reactions to the poems. One day, I was reading Longfellow's poem about swinging "up so high", One woman smiled and commented, "I remember that one." On another occasion in April, I was at the Emerald Ridge Nursing Home. Eight people came for our poetry reading and seven seemed interested. One man sat in a wheelchair, slumped forward and bent over, showing no reactions to the poems we were reading. Our last poem was "Casey at the Bat" and we had chosen it because it was spring and the baseball season had just begun. I was reading about Casey stepping to the plate and facing the opposing pitcher. Suddenly, the man who seemed to be sleepy or disinterested, sat up. He was alert and was saying the words along with me. As volunteers, we don't expect to be paid but this man's positive reaction to "Casey at the Bat" was like giving me a day's pay.

Another activity of The Autumn Players was presenting stories to children through the method of reader's theater. We sat on a stage facing the girls and boys and read stories that were of special interest to them. We had the pages in a loose-leaf notebook and the book was propped up before us on a music stand. We could look down to read the script, then we'd look up as we read the story. We used our hands and bodies to give action to what we were reading and we showed emotions on our faces. This was very effective as we read Rudyard Kipling's story, "How the Camel Got His Hump" and Dr. Seuss's story, "And To Think That I Saw It on Mulberry Street". We did reader's theater at the Haw Creek Elementary School, at the Venable School in Candler, at the Weaverville Elementary, and at several other schools.

Interesting Encounters

When Ruth and I left New York City in 1972, we moved to Vermont and then to North Carolina in 1991. In these two states which are much smaller than New York, we came to meet people who were known in literature, in athletics, in politics, and in entertainment: Some of these people are Madeleine KUNIN (1895-1991), Richard SNELLING, Bernard SANDERS, Patrick LEAHY, Harry GOLDEN, Carl Sandburg, and Bob TERRELL.

The names I've just mentioned are of people you might approach with respect and with dignity. The reality is that they are not formal at all and it is common for them to address you by first name and for you to do the same with them. Governor Richard Snelling, when you meet him, becomes Dick, Senator Bernard Sanders becomes Bernie, Senator Patrick Leahy becomes Pat and Bob Terrell, the well-known writer for the *Asheville Citizen Times* was only Bob. Because of the informality, I feel comfortable using many of their anecdotes and stories when I have gone to some group or organization as a guest speaker.

Madeleine KUNIN became the Governor of Vermont in 1985. Early in the 1970's, she ran for a position in the State House of Representatives and she campaigned throughout the state so people would have a chance to meet her. When she came to Rutland, she came to our house on Meadowbrook Road for an afternoon tea. We invited our neighbors for tea and for a chance to meet Mrs. Kunin. Twenty-five people came for this event and listened to Madeleine's speech. She was elected to the State House, and was so effective as a representative that she became the Governor. Ruth and I supported her whenever we could because we felt she was correct in trying to improve the environment and to help senior citizens of Vermont who had health problems.

Allen at the office of Madeleine Kunin, former Govenor of Vermont

Richard SNELLING was the Governor from 1972-1985. He supported the idea of physical fitness and told us that there was a room with a treadmill and other exercise machines just next to his office in Montpelier. Dick helped the Parks and Recreation Department establish the Green Mountain Senior Games. As the Governor, he would go to different parts of Vermont on official business. He had an appointment secretary and if you knew that Dick was coming to your area, it was possible that he'd come to your group to make a speech, have lunch or dinner with your organization, or get to see some place that needed his attention. Every summer, the governor would come to the Snowshed Lodge on Killington Mountain to attend the Governor's Picnic for Senior Citizens. There would be no snow on the mountain during the summer and there were no ski people there to use the facilities. At the governor's invitation, hundreds of senior citizens would come to this picnic. There was food, music, games, and I was there to lead the people in folk and square dancing. They would also have fun with a spelling contest and I would be the Pronouncer, creating an event that was exciting for the spellers and fun for the audience. Dick Snelling would always come to the picnic, walking among the tables, shaking hands with the seniors and encouraging everyone to have a good time. I had a good time, too, because I earned a day's pay as a recreation leader.

Bernard SANDERS was the Mayor of Burlington. He was a socialist and did his best to help the poor people of the area. I recall meeting Bernie at the Tunbridge Fair where he was shaking hands with people and electioneering for a higher office.

Patrick LEAHY is a U.S. Senator from Vermont and he became a powerful democrat in Washington, DC. In 1978, I asked him for help when we were trying to obtain a caboose for the Sugar Maple Children's Center. We did obtain a caboose from the Delaware and Hudson Railroad and on August 6, 1978, Pat himself could not be with us as we moved the caboose from the train yard to Sugar Maple, but he had asked his wife to be there with us. I recall chatting with her as the caboose was making its way along Main Street.

In North Carolina, Zebulon VANCE (1830-1894) was a well-known and very effective lawyer. During the Civil War, he became a colonel and then had to leave his regiment when he was elected governor. He became a representative in Washington, DC and then was elected as senator, a post that he kept until he died in 1894. People named their boys Zebulon and there is a city 20 miles east of Raleigh named Zebulon. Vance was a very eloquent orator and a persuasive speaker and this ability helped him to rule the state of North Carolina during and after the Civil War. He would often tell a joke to lighten the audiences and he felt that mirth does for the soul what sleep does for the body. This anecdote tells of Vance's interest in the people of Western North Caro-

143

lina:

Abby HOUSER of Franklin, NC had a fine reputation for caring for soldiers who were wounded in the Civil War. In 1890, she wanted to see Senator Vance about her husband's pension from the Mexican War. Zeb wrote her a ticket for transportation:

TO ALL RAILROAD OFFICIALS: PLEASE PASS ABBY HOUSER TO AND FROM WASHINGTON, DC ON OFFICIAL BUSINESS.

Nobody rejected this pass written on official stationery and signed by U.S. Senator Zebulon Vance. He arranged for Abby to see President Benjamin Harrison. Harrison listened to her and then told her to leave the pension application with him, to be processed. "No sir", protested Abby, "I am not going to leave a valuable document in the hands of a Republican." Senator Vance told her not to worry and that her request would be approved. Abby was satisfied and returned to Franklin, using Zeb's pass.

Harry GOLDEN was born in Galicia, Austria in 1902. He came to the U.S. in 1905 with his mother and two sisters and the Golden family lived at 171 Eldridge Street on the Lower East Side of New York City. He went to Public School #20, a school for boys only, and started there at age six. Harry loved reading and read everything he could about Americans and English history. He did well in school and when he brought his report card home with all A's, his mother would show the card to all the neighbors. He helped his mother when they went shopping at a market under the Williamsburg Bridge, eight blocks away. Harry joined the Young People's Socialist League in 1917 at the age of 15. He was familiar with the pamphlets of Carl SANDBURG and Eugene V. DEBS and he believed in them.

In the middle of 1938, Harry Golden got a job at the *New York Daily Mirror*, working as a reporter and selling advertising for the paper. A newspaper in Norfolk, VA offered him more money so Harry moved to Virginia and then, in 1941, to Charlotte, NC, selling ads and writing editorials for the *Charlotte Observer*. Harry Golden met Carl Sandburg for the first time in 1948 when Sandburg was to do a program at Davidson College. They became good friends even though Carl was twenty years older. Harry would often drive to Sandburg's house in Flat Rock for conversations.

A book publisher in New York City liked the pieces that Harry Golden had written in his book, *Only in America*. They said they would print 10,000 copies by July 27, 1958. On that morning, it developed that the newspaper reviews were all favorable. By noon, the phones were ringing with large re-orders. The U.S. Army ordered 900 copies for its libraries all over the U.S. They sold 300,000 copies in hardback and when Pocket Books printed it as a paperback, it brought in additional success stories. I have one of the paperback copies, published in July 1958, and on the cover is printed the price: 50 cents. The book has a Foreword written by Carl Sandburg.

In 1972, Harry Golden assembled a book that he called *The Golden Book of Jewish Humor*. He mentions Heinrich HEINE, a German Poet (1797-1856) who was reading in a public library in Paris. Two women at the next table were chattering and gossiping for about 15 minutes. He was annoyed and finally, he leaned over and asked, "Excuse me, ladies, but does my reading interfere with your conversation?"

> At a religious school, the teacher asked one of his students, "Yussele, do you say your prayers before each meal?"No, Melamed", the boy said to his teacher. "What? You don't pray before each meal?"
> " I don't have to. My mother's a good cook".

About 40 years ago in Chicago, the Transit Authority let people buy a monthly pass to ride on the buses or trains. Arnold GREENBERG tells of his parents who lived in Skokie, IL, next door to the McCarthy family. One Saturday, Minnie Greenberg borrowed Mary McCarthy's commuter ticket to go to downtown Chicago. On the trains, a stern-looking conductor, in uniform, looked at Minnie Greenberg and saw the name Mary McCarthy on the ticket. He gave her a blank ticket and asked her to sign her name. Mrs. Greenberg looked at the conductor and huffed, "I'm sorry, General, but on Saturday I never write."

Oscar LEVANT, the famous pianist and entertainer, called his mother one day. He told her he had been going with a girl, he had proposed to her, and she had accepted. "All right, Oscar. That's good. I'm glad to hear it. Did you practice your piano today?"

Harry Golden felt that the friendship with Carl Sandburg was "the most rewarding of my life". I deemed him a great American writer for his pamphlets on Socialism, for his biography of Abraham Lincoln, and for his poem about the Depression, "The People, Yes". Sandburg broke with the Socialists because he supported the U.S. in World War I against Germany, and in 1940, he lectured in support of the U.S. action against the Nazis of Europe. Since 1917, Sandburg was a political independent. He was an active supporter of the Democratic Party and he campaigned vigorously for Franklin Delano Roosevelt in each of his four campaigns. He also campaigned for John F. Kennedy in 1960. Harry Golden says Sandburg had a professional understanding of politics, social and cultural problems.

Carl Sandburg called his throat the voice box and he had all sorts of mufflers that he wrapped around his neck when he went out for a walk. The throat was very important to him because that's what he needed to produce income from his lectures and songs.

Sam Ervin used to say, "That reminds me of a stoh-ree". In May of 1980, I was planning a Walk for Fitness as an activity of the Governor's Council on Physical Fitness. I had studied the map of Vermont and I thought it would be a challenging and colorful walk to start at the City Hall of Middlebury and walk on country roads through dairy pastures, and through a covered bridge. Walking a round trip of five miles would take you past the Morgan Horse Farm, where there was a statue of a Morgan Horse. To finish the walk, you went through a Covered Bridge that took you over the Middlebury River. This was an unusual bridge, because while most covered bridges are one lane wide, this bridge was two lanes wide and there was also a walkway for pedestrians to protect them from the traffic. Just in case people did not want to walk all five miles, I had a shorter three mile loop which still ended with a walk through the covered bridge. And just in case people did not want to walk three miles, I had planned a one-mile loop. This, too, ended with walkers going through the covered bridge. In order to plan this walk, I studied the rural areas on a big map and to be sure all was correct, I planned to do a walk-through on February 16. It was a cold day in Rutland but I prepared for the walk with a few layers of clothing, thermal underwear, a woolen shirt, ear muffs, cap, gloves, a scarf and high shoes for walking on snow. There was no trouble driving the 32 miles to Middlebury on U.S. 7, and parking next to the City Hall. It was cold, 14 degrees below zero and windy, but I had come prepared for the walk and I wasn't going to let the weather deter me.

I started on the five mile loop but I found the wind to be fierce and there was nothing to protect my face. As I walked, I took the muffler from around my neck and wrapped it around my face, just below eye level. I continued to walk but I encountered a new problem. Although the muffler covered my nose, I was able to breathe but as the warm air came out of my nostrils, it met the

VERMONT LAND CRUISES......

"Through the Beautiful Green Mountains"

— 1986 SEASON —

Lamoille Valley Railroad

STAFFORD AVENUE
MORRISVILLE, VERMONT 05661
802-888-4255

147

cold air of the 14 below zero condition. The cold air condensed my warm breath and I found that my nose was dripping into the muffler. The muffler became wet from the dripping and the frigid air caused the drips to freeze and as I looked down, I could see icicles hanging from the muffler. As I regarded this predicament, I had a brief consultation with myself and I changed my plans from the five mile walk to a one mile walk. I made it through the covered bridge, to my car, and to the nearest diner for some hot coffee.

Vermont has about 100 covered bridges and while they are picturesque, they are functional. People use them to cross rivers and streams and the bridges are sturdy enough for horses and wagons, automobiles, and small trucks. There is only one covered bridge for railroads and that is used by the Lamoille Valley Railroad as it goes between the towns of Woolcott and Hardwick. This bridge is a historic landmark and is one of the last covered railroad bridges in the U.S.

When Carl Sandburg was 21 years old, he traveled as a hobo to different parts of the country. Returning to Illinois, he hopped a freight train one night, going west out of Philadelphia. The next morning, he was in Pittsburgh. In the afternoon, he was in an empty gondola car with five other hobos. Two constables climbed into the car and arrested all six men. They were handcuffed, two by two, and brought before a judge, charged with "riding on a railroad train without a ticket". Carl Sandburg explained that he was a veteran of the Spanish-American War and had been with the army in Puerto Rico. The judge said, "Ten dollars or ten days". Sandburg served the ten days and hopped freight trains back to Chicago.

Afterward, Carl thought he could sue Allegheny County for false arrest. The charge was "riding on a railroad train without a ticket". His premise: 1) The coal car was not part of a passenger train, and 2) the car was not moving while they were in it and the charge was that they were riding.

Carl Sandburg was a work-a-holic. In doing research, he worked 16-18 hours per day. Sometimes, he'd have a severe headache and he thought, "Is this a symptom of cerebral hemorrhage?" A little prayer came to him: "O Lord, if thou wilt permit me to finish this task, then thou mayest have me". In 1939, Sandburg finished his famous book, *Abraham Lincoln: The War Years*. He had worked on it for eleven years and it was not only a biography of Lincoln but a history of his administration and of the Civil War as well. It was in four volumes and in 1940, he received the Pulitzer Prize in History for this work. On Lincoln's Birthday in 1959, Sandburg addressed a joint session of Congress, members of the Supreme Court, and the Cabinet.

Edward R. MURROW came to Connemara in 1954 to tape material for a television program on Carl Sandburg. He asked Sandburg, "What do you think is the worst word in the English language?" Carl answered, "The one word more detestable than any other is EXCLOOOSIVE. When you're exclooosive, you shut people out and a large range of humanity is lost from your head and heart".

Sandburg liked to eat oranges – peelings and all. He was proud of the way he ate oranges. As a child, his hard-working parents on special occasions would give to each child in the family a 5 cent bag of candy and a 5 cent orange. He honored this fruit by eating all of the inside, pulp and peelings.

The Sandburg Family lived in Galesburg, IL and there were seven children in the family. They bought their groceries from Swan Olson's Store and one of the family would go to the store, buy what Mrs. Sandburg wanted and tell Swan OLSON to "put it in the book". Carl's father worked for the Chicago, Burlington, and Quincy Railroad and once a month, he would cash his check and settle the account. When Carl reached an age where he could be trusted with THE BOOK, Mrs. Sandburg sent him to the store one day with a note for molasses and pancake flour. Carl handed over the book and Swan Olson entered the amount. Carl saw that he could buy something for himself because the grocer would put it in the book. He bought 5 cents worth of licorice and had Mr. Olson put it in the book. When he reached home, Carl's mother saw that his face and hands were smeared with licorice. She asked him where he got the licorice and he said he told Mr. Olson to put it on the book. She gave him a good beating and he learned that the book was for the family, not for him.

In 1929, when my parents had a dry goods store in Williamsburg, they had customers who bought clothing and said, "Put it on the book". When the Depression came, people didn't have money to pay their accounts and my folks didn't have money to pay their bills. Life was hard for everybody in those days.

In 1919, Carl Sandburg and his wife, Paula, lived in Elmhurst, IL. They had three children: Margaret, age 10, Janet, age 5, and Helga, age 3 + . Carl would come home from work and make up stories for the three girls. He told them about a blue fox that lived beneath the front porch of their home. The fox would come into the house through an open kitchen window to drink cream from a saucer. The fox would measure himself between sips to be sure he could get out again. The girls would run to their daddy and beg him to, "Tell me a fox. Tell me a fox". Sandburg invented more tales and these became the *Rootabaga Stories*, published in 1922.

Sandburg made up his own fairy tales. He created characters that lived in the middle west where one of the most important crops was corn. He wrote nothing to frighten children. Carl called his imaginary people CORNFAIRIES and he created unusual names for the people in his stories, with names like:

> The girls, Blixie, Bimber
>
> The Potato Face Blind Man
>
> The Village of Liver-and-Onions
>
> A hen called Shush Shush
>
> A girl, Deep Red Roses, who loved and was left by three men:
> Shoulder Straps, High High Over, and Six Bits

The stories have a spirit of play and simplicity and they run the gamut from comedy to tragedy. Sandburg plays with the alphabet and uses alliteration and euphony. Blixie and Bimber fell in love with men who had an X in their names: Silas Baxby, Fritz Axenbax, and James Sixbixdix. Henry Hagglyhoagly serenades Susan Slackentwist.

Paula Steinburg went to the Rosa Edwards Public School in Hendersonville, NC. When Paula was in Grade 2, the principal asked Carl Sandburg to give a reading of the *Rootabaga Stories* to the 3rd and 4th grade assembly. He did so with his deep love for fantasy and language.

When Sandburg's daughter, Helga, grew up, she entered family conversations. If they were telling jokes, she would relate one that she knew. She told a story about a little boy named Steve in New York City. He loved the statue of General Grant on his horse in a park in Upper Manhattan. One day, Steve's mother said they had to leave New York City because daddy had a job in another city. Steve went to the statue as often as he could. The day before they were going to move, his mother said, "Take one last look and then we really must go". They stood there looking and then Steve said, "Mama, who is the man on General Grant?"

On June 6, 1963, when Carl Sandburg was 85 years old, Harcourt, Brace & World, Sandburg's publisher since 1919, arranged a party for him. It was at the Waldorf Astoria Hotel and it celebrated a double good fortune: Carl's 85th Birthday and the publication of his new volume of poems, *Honey and Salt*. It was a deluxe dinner and there were 108 guests. After dinner, the speeches were short and Sandburg's was the shortest. The guests lined up before Sandburg, each with a copy of *Honey and Salt*, waiting for him to write an inscription. He could not remember the names of some people and he'd say, "Just how do you spell your name?" Carl commented, "I am not proud of my FORGETTERY nor do I hang my head in shame. Thankfully, a lapse is not a loss. A candle always burns in the mind's window. Sooner or later, there is a ring of the doorbell and it is the wandering

151

memory come home again".

A literary columnist had put the name of Carl Sandburg on a list of North Carolina writers. Someone disputed this, saying that Sandburg was born in Illinois and lived most of his life in Illinois and Michigan. Sandburg became indignant, saying, "I pay my taxes here. I shall die here. I am a North Carolina writer".

Another person from North Carolina who has been helpful to me as a guest speaker is Bob TERRELL. Bob Terrell was born at home, in Addie, North Carolina, about five miles east of Sylva, NC. Addie was small with a population of 200, but it had a community school where everyone was able to walk to attend. Bob had friends who liked to play cowboys using stick horses. They played marbles, rolled hoops and listened on the radio to The Lone Ranger. On Saturdays, he'd go into Sylva to see western movies where admission was 10 cents. Bob went to high school in Sylva in 1941. He was good at writing but he was very nervous when he had to stand up and make a speech in class. I recall feeling the same way when I had to make a speech in high school and I had the same insecurity when I attended classes at Brooklyn College. Since I wanted to become a teacher, I had to take several courses in Education and when I did student teaching in Latin at James Madison High School, I felt I knew the subject matter and my nervousness disappeared.

Bob Terrell was a sports writer for his college newspaper and for *The Sylva Herald*. He says that he was a fast writer and a very fast typist. He knew what career he wanted and he became a writer for newspapers as well as a writer of over 45 books. In 1949, he accepted a job with *The Citizen* in Asheville. He covered the sports of Asheville and often wrote columns and books that made people chuckle. In 1956, he became the sports editor and covered the games of the Asheville Tourists. As a guest speaker, he would remember anecdotes and include them in his remarks. One day, in talking to the Kiwanis Club of Asheville, he told us about his uncle, Randy Crawford, who was to celebrate his 100th birthday. Bob drove from Asheville to Addie to spend a little time with his uncle. Bob asked him, "How come you lived to 100?" Uncle Randy answered, "I ain't dead yet". Bob countered with, "Can you give a hint to other people on how to have a long life? I'd like to print that in my column in the paper". "Well", said Uncle Randy, "I didn't gamble. I didn't drink. I didn't fool around with women. I did smoke cigarettes, though, but I stopped two years ago". Bob followed up on this, "Why did you stop smoking at 98?" Uncle Randy explained, "As we become older, we become forgetful. One day, I put a cigarette in my mouth, lit a wooden match and forgot what to do with it. The match burned down to my fingers and then I remembered why I had lit it. That's when I decided to stop smoking".

In 1954, Bob Terrell was covering a game of the Asheville Tourists at McCormick Field. He had to remain in the Press Box to finish the statistics before going back to the *Asheville Citizen-Times* to write up the game. He hadn't finished when the custodian turned off the field lights. There must have been a million bugs flying around those lights and when the lights were turned off, they all came flying to the Press Box lights. They flew around and around Bob's head and he felt something in his right ear as if someone had hit him with a bat. He reached for his ear and without realizing it, he pushed a huge moth into his ear and he could feel the moth flapping its wings. He called the paper and said he would leave the scorebook on the hood of his car because he was going to the hospital. In the dressing room, the trainer looked at the ear but the moth was out of sight. He drove Bob to Mission Memorial Hospital to the Emergency Room. A nurse said she could handle it. She poured some warm liquid into his ear. This drowned the moth and she was able to use medical tweezers to pull it out.

Another of Bob Terrell's stories tells of a baseball game in 1962 between the Asheville Tourists and the Macon Peaches, a farm team of the Cincinnati Reds. Pete Rose played second base for the Macon Peaches and he was a good hitter, even then. Pete came to bat in the top of the ninth, two-out, and bases loaded. The

Tourists were leading by one run, with the score 5 to 4. The count on Pete Rose went to 3 and 2. A walk would tie the game and a hit by Pete would put the Peaches ahead. Pete Rose was really a threat to the Tourists. The manager of the Tourists, Ray Hathaway, called time and walked to the mound. The catcher of the Tourists also walked to the mound for a conference of three. After a quick discussion, Ray Hathaway returned to the dugout and the catcher took his position behind the plate. The catcher didn't squat in his usual position. He stood upright and extended his right arm to the right, a sign calling for ball 4 and an intentional walk. Pete Rose relaxed, willing to take the walk and tie the score. Tom Butters, the Asheville pitcher, without a windup, threw a strike right down the middle and caught Pete Rose looking. The strategy worked and the Asheville Tourists won the game.

CHAPTER 16

Approaching the End of the Line

The ninety two years since 1921 have been epochal with the Era of the Depression, the presidency of Franklin D. Roosevelt, World War II, and the dropping of the atom bomb. I have mentioned when my son, Steve, was born in 1948 and we puzzled over who would carry him out of the Long Island College Hospital. Steve and his wife Anita, live in North Potomac, MD and they have two children, Allison and Marc. Allison, my granddaughter, has two children, Gregory, my Great-Grandson, and Molly, my Great Grand-Daughter. Marc, my grandson, and his wife, Celia, are both attorneys and live and work in Washington, DC. Their son, Nate (the Great) was born on December 26, 2010 and is my second Great-Grandson.

My Daughter-in-law Anita, with my Grand-daughter Allison and Great Grandson Greg

My son Steve, with Molly, my Great Granddaughter

We also puzzled over Dory's blood when she was born in 1951 at the Kew Gardens Hospital. Because I was blood type A+ and my wife, Ruth, was O-, our daughter was liable to jaundice when she was born. The doctor recommended a blood

My Daughter Dory With her husband Paul

transfusion and our daughter, Dory, one day old, had a complete transfusion. She received a full supply of A+ blood. Dory pulled through this serious procedure and made it for 57 years. She passed away on May 15, 2008 in Berkeley, CA, because of cancer in the stomach. Dory and her husband, Paul Gruber, had one daughter, Emily, in 1982. Emily is married to Guy Somberg and they live in El Cerrito, CA. I was so proud of Emily when she participated in the Avon-Walk-For-Cancer, a two-day thirty nine mile trek. She has done this for three years, always thinking of what her mother had done for her.

Another special day in my life was Saturday, May 29, 2009. The Rotary Club of Asheville had planned an "Honor Air Flight" to thank

My Granddaughter Emily with her husband Guy

156

World War II veterans for service to their country. They chartered an airplane, and had it ready and waiting for us at the Asheville Airport. Before we boarded, Joyce MILLER introduced herself to Wayne Montgomery, Howard Pinner, and me. She said she would be our guide for the entire trip and would help us if we needed anything.

Allen & Asheville area Veterans board the Honor Air Flight, Asheville, NC Airport

We left Asheville at 10 A.M. and landed at Washington, DC

Wayne Montgomery, Howard Pinner, and Allen ready for take-off, Asheville, NC airport

157

at 11:30 A.M. There were three special buses waiting for us with policemen on motorcycles to provide a non-stop drive to the area of the war memorials. On the Mall near the Lincoln Memorial, we saw the Korean-War Veteran's Memorial, 19 stainless steel sculptures of US soldiers on patrol.

The Korean War Veteran's Memorial, Washington, DC

We walked alongside the Vietnam Memorial Wall, a most impressive wall of shiny black granite with the names inscribed of all soldiers killed or missing in action in the Vietnam War. A box lunch was ready for us under a big tent and while we were eating, Bob DOLE and his wife, Elizabeth, circulated, greeting and chatting with the veterans. Bob Dole, a Republican from Kansas, ran for President of the United States against Bill CLINTON in the election of 1996. Dole lost to Clinton and his democratic Vice President, Al GORE. After lunch, Bob Dole greeted us with a short speech and he and his wife, Elizabeth, spent more time speaking with the veterans. Elizabeth was very cordial, smiled a lot, and felt comfortable with us since she comes from Salisbury, NC, and was a U.S. Senator from North Carolina from 2003 – 2009.

After lunch, we walked to the Marine Corps War Memorial where there is the famous statue of U.S. Marines raising the flag on Iwo Jima in 1945. Photographer Joe ROSENTHAL took a picture of the six marines raising the U.S. flag. This picture is so dramatic that Rosenthal won a Pulitzer Prize in 1945 for his work.

Near this statue is the National World War II Memorial.

The Marine Corps War Memorial, Washington, DC

There are 56 pillars surrounding a pool and plaza that represent the District of Columbia, and the state and territories of the World War II period. A curved wall is covered with gold stars representing those who died in this war. From the mall, we could see the Lincoln Memorial and the Washington Monument. At 4 P.M., we went to the Tomb of the Unknown Soldier and were there to see the changing of the guard. We who were soldiers certainly appreciate the men who guard the tomb and who patrol the area meticulously. We returned to our buses for a guided tour of the District of Columbia. There was a professional guide who explained many of the important buildings and places of interest, including Arlington Cemetery. The buses took us to the Washington Airport and we landed in Asheville at 7 P.M.

What an arrival we had! As we left the plane and walked through the lobby of the airport, we met a huge crowd of people who greeted us. There were teenagers in uniform of the Civil Air Patrol, members of the R.O.T.C. in uniform, hundreds of people waving flags, holding balloons, and signs saying, "Thank You". There was a band playing music to welcome us and as we walked through the crowd, people were saluting us and reaching out to touch us. This reception in 2009 was 64 years after World War II ended and it was an exciting and thrilling greeting to those of us who had been in World War II. On June 2, just four days after the Honor Air Flight, I received a heavy brown envelope from our Rotary guide, Joyce Miller. She sent me copies of pictures she had taken in Asheville, on the plane, and in Washington. There were 93 color pictures of our trip and I shall treasure them forever.

As you grow older, you have experiences that are similar to ones you have had earlier in life. In May of 2011, a new building at Congregation Beth Ha Tephila, here in Asheville, was celebrated. Our President, Larry WEISS, and the Finance Committee worked very hard to obtain donations for the construction of the new building. Larry and Joe KARPEN made appeals showing how much the building would cost, the money people had donated, and what remained to complete the financing. They were successful, and on May 16, 2011, there was a groundbreaking ceremony at the corner of Liberty and Broad Streets, Asheville, NC, and the contractor began work. As of this writing, August 11, 2012, much of the work has been done and we are looking forward to the weekend of December 14, 2012 for the dedication of the new building.

I look back to 1965 when our congregation, Temple Beth El of Laurelton, had a campaign to erect a new building on 233rd Street, in Laurelton, Long Island. We had a groundbreaking ceremony on February 7, 1965 and a consecration and dedication of the new building on December 15, 1967. I was the president of the congregation at that time and I see the similarity of what we are doing now to what we did 47 years ago.

Yes, we are slowing down and I guess that is to be expected

when you reach the age of 90. I thought of that two weeks ago, on Thursday, August 2, 2012 as I was in the Diana Wortham Theatre in Asheville, watching the Asheville Dance and Folk Festival. I sat in the balcony admiring the groups of dancers doing their clogging, square dancing, and smooth dancing, and thinking back to August 3, 2006. At that time, I was on the Diana Wortham stage with the group from the College for Seniors doing our smooth dancing routine. Earlier this year, on May 17, I participated in the Senior Games of Buncombe County. I competed in croquet, horseshoes, shuffleboard, and billiards. At the awards ceremony, Dee BLACK, Director of the Senior Games, gave me a gold medal for being first in my age group in these events. I also received a commendation for this poem which I submitted as an entry in the Literary Arts Competition.

Silver Arts Showcase, Sub category: Poetry
Verses on the Senior Games May 22, 2012

Horseshoes
In my right hand, I hold the shoe,
Take aim at the stake and throw it true.
Hope it's a ringer or close to the post,
That will give me some points, what I want most.

Billiards
Fifteen balls on the table, some close, some apart,
With cue stick in my hand, I shoot with a prayer in my heart
That the cue ball will travel, swiftly, with skill,
Will sink number five, not miss like a pill.

Croquet
If I hit the ball and it goes through the wicket,
I have another shot; it's like a free ticket,
And if my play hits the other man's ball,
I shoot again and hope I won't stall.

Shuffleboard
I hold the stick; aim the disc with care,

161

Hoping it will go in the ten point square.
If it does, I feel like a champ, just great
'Til my opponent knocks it out, that's my fate.

As the years pass, we watch our children mature, marry and have children of their own. Every November, my Granddaughter Emily, her husband Guy, and father-in-law Paul Gruber fly to Asheville to spend a few days with me. I stay in touch with Steve and Anita's family too, their two children, Allison and Marc, and my Great Grandchildren Gregory and Molly. Marc and Celia stay busy in Washington, DC, especially with two

My Great Grandson 'Nate the Great'

year old Nate to keep them on their toes. On February 28th, 2013, Celia and Marc welcomed my third Great-Grandson, Charles Alexander Sher, into the world.

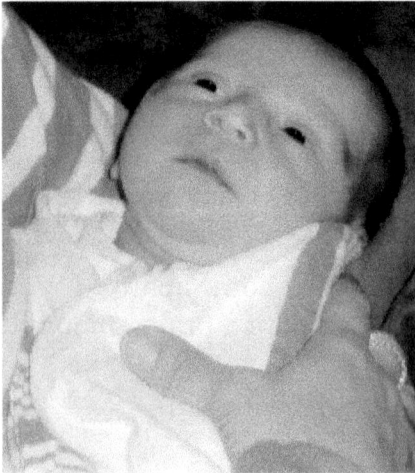

My newest Great Grandson, Charles Alexander

We write to one another, and speak on the telephone but I hadn't gone up north to see them. On November 29, 2012, I did drive up to Gaithersburg, MD and was able to spend a few days with this part of our family. The three Great Grandchildren ages 7, 5 and 2 are very, very active. They all came to Steve and Anita's house in North Potomac, MD on Saturday and the three

children immediately began playing with toys, running around the house, and then going outside to ride scooters and play ball. At my age of 91, I sat back and watched them at play, marveling at how busy they were. On Saturday evening, all nine of us went to an Italian restaurant for dinner. The children were all good eaters and it was a delight to spend the evening with them.

Allison had brought a deck of cards with their toys and Gregory and Molly played Slap Jack. I watched them play and when the game ended, there was an argument over who won. I resolved the controversy by joining them in a three handed game of Slap Jack. This settled all disputes and when they tired of Slap Jack, I taught them a new card game, a simplified form of Casino. This was a novelty for Gregory and Molly because I don't think they regarded Grandpa Allen as one who could teach them anything. We played three games of Casino and I'm sure they will be playing it when they are home in Lafayette Hill.

Marc and Celia went home on Saturday with two-year old Nate, and Allison left for home on Sunday afternoon with Greg and Molly. I am sure that Anita and Steve heaved a sigh of relief when their house was quiet and they could relax. Gaithersburg is 500 miles from Asheville and I drove home in two days, staying overnight at a motel in Roanoke, VA. This visit with the family was a delightful experience and my time with the Great Grandchildren will be a forever memory.

Watching our family expand as weddings occurred has brought me great happiness, and I have enjoyed receiving invitations to attend the ceremonies. In 1997, a grand-nephew, Michael Hertz, was married in Bowie, MD. I flew to Washington, DC and then rented a car to drive to Bowie. Michael and his new wife, Shannon, were very cordial to me as were other relatives who were there. Despite greetings by the friends and family, I felt a certain loneliness in being at the wedding alone.

On July 18, 2009, my grandson, Marc Sher, was married to Celia Martellino in Newport, RI. I flew to Providence and then drove to their synagogue in Newport. Marc and Celia asked me to be part of the procession as they walked down the aisle. During the ceremony and the festivities afterwards, I tried to be cheerful but again, there was the feeling of being alone. Six weeks later, Josh Kaufman, a grand-nephew, was married in Rockville, MD. I planned to drive there in two days, staying overnight at a motel in Norfolk, VA. This city is the headquarters of the Norfolk Southern Railroad and the company has a railroad museum there. I drove to the museum and had a happy experience seeing the locomotives and passenger cars that were on display. There was a shop that sold railroad souvenirs and I brought home a few items that I still enjoy. My sister, Florence, had come from Miami Beach to this wedding as well as her daughter, Sarah Stafford, from Brooklyn, NY. It was a great pleasure to be with them and catch up on family news.

This wedding was on the Sunday of Labor Day Weekend. Because so many people travel on those days, the police warned drivers to be careful and obey the speed limits. "Speeding causes accidents", the patrolmen warned. As I drove on the highway and on the interstates, I used the cruise control. Whatever the speed limit was, I set the cruise control at only 5 miles above the limit. On the northbound and southbound highways, I saw many police cars on patrol. Furthermore, I saw policemen at the side of the road, giving tickets to speeders. It was 500 miles from Rockville, MD to Asheville and I did it in one day, reaching home safely by 7 P.M.

My granddaughter, Emily, lived in Berkeley, CA and attended the University of Puget Sound. She met Guy Somberg, and they were married on March 7, 2012 in the catering facilities of the Oakland Zoo. The ceremony took place outdoors and I had the honor of holding one of the poles that supported their wedding canopy. They now live in El Cerrito, CA, 2,000 miles from Asheville. This past November 22nd, my 91st birthday, arrived on Thanksgiving Day. With Emily, Guy, and her father-in-law Paul, it was a sincere occasion to give "Thanks" for a visit by my western family to acknowledge my ninety first birthday.

My Railroad Ticket Hasn't Expired Yet

I don't know how much longer I'll live. It is with a feeling of assurance, however, that I know I'll be buried together with other distinguished people of "the Old North State" in the Riverside Cemetery, often called 'The Westminster Abbey of the South'.

Riverside Cemetery in Asheville is a historic site in the State of North Carolina. Visitors come to this cemetery to see the graves of these well-known Carolinians:

Thomas CLINGMAN – a general in the Confederate Army, a U.S. Congressman and a U.S. Senator. He was a mountain climber and a geologist and he measured Clingman's Dome to be 6,642', only 42 feet shorter than Mount Mitchell.

Isaac DICKSON – an educator who worked hard so that Asheville schools would benefit African-American children. His name is remembered by the school on Hill Street, which is called the Isaac Dickson Elementary School.

Solomon LIPINSKY – a merchant of Asheville who founded Bon Marche', one of the largest department stores in Western North Carolina. He was a philanthropist and donated money to UNC-A. The Lipinsky Auditorium was named in his honor.

O.Henry / William Sydney Porter (1862-1910) – is the pen name of William Sydney Porter. He was a prolific writer of short stories, many of which build up to sharp, unexpected endings. He was born in Greensboro, NC, and worked in his uncle's drugstore. Then he moved to Austin, TX where he worked as a bank clerk. He spent three years in prison for embezzling funds.

Zebulon Baird VANCE (1830-1894) – served in the Civil War as a colonel and served twice as a governor of North Carolina. He was a member of the House of Representatives, and also a member of the U.S. Senate. The Vance Monument in downtown Asheville is a memorial to him, and his statue is in Statuary Hall, in Washington, DC.

Thomas WOLFE (1908-1938)- an author born in Asheville, NC who wrote his first novel about Asheville at the turn of the century, *Look Homeward Angel*, in 1929. He is famous for his autobiographical novels. His second novel, published in 1935 was *Of Time and the River*.

My wife, Ruth, died in 1996 and is buried in Riverside Cemetery. I have reserved the plot next to hers for myself. As I write

165

this in 2013, at the age of 91, I look back fondly on a full life. If anyone is thinking of an epitaph, here are three by Richard LEDERER in his article, "Tomb It May Concern":

For a railroad conductor – THIS IS THE END OF THE LINE
For a caterer – THIS IS MY LAST AFFAIR
For a dentist – I'VE FILLED MY LAST CAVITY.

Allen died peacefully in his sleep the evening of May 2nd, 2013, content with the knowledge he had achieved his dream of writing this book.

Index of Photographs & Articles

167

168

www.ingramcontent.com/pod-product-compliance
Lightning Source LLC
LaVergne TN
LVHW021450080426
835509LV00018B/2227